THE MAIN PRINCIPLES

These are the three key ideas that we should focus on when thinking about cooking sustainably

ZERO WASTE

ORGANIC AND SEASONAL

50% OF PRODUCE WITHIN 30 MILES

THANK YOU

All my love to my Mum and Dad, thank you for everything. My brothers, my best friends. My family, you are the core. Thank you Kirsten, for opening my eyes in Florence. Tommaso – the best olive oil in the world and your friendship. Rannuccio and Gilda, your extreme, crazy and dedicated vision. To Tye Rock, a place for everyone where food was central. To Hungerford Park, a place of rare beauty. To Italy, my other life. To South America for your extraordinary beauty – a reason why sustainability is so important. To Nothing But The Grape, for that first real understanding of how important organic culture is, and why the land is the most important asset. Thank you to the Sustainable Restaurant Association, for your help and for continually raising the bar. Thank you to the hospitality industry for the wonderful and amazing sensations that you continue to offer, thank you for giving. Thank you to Jamie Oliver for that first seed of inspiration. Thank you to everyone who has ever been a part of The Wheatsheaf. Thank you to Steph, my editor for saying yes, and your massive support. And thank you to all at Pavilion, especially Katie, Helen and Amy, for all the incredible energy, belief and work on this book. To Evi-O.Studio, Evi O., Susan Le and Nicole Ho, and the photography team Louise Hagger, Seiko Hatfield and Rachel Vere. And finally, thank you to everyone who reads this book and passes the message on... together we will make the difference.

To Lauren and Patebu, all the love in the world. Everything. Our adventure continues...

NOTES

This book was produced ecologically using a waterless printing process in compliance with the objectives of the Environmental Protection Agency.

All the ingredients used in these recipes should be organic and locally sourced as much as possible. Or use up what you have rather than going out to buy something new.

When foraging for wild food, you must be able to correctly identify what you are picking, otherwise you should not eat it.

All eggs are medium (UK) or large (US). Uncooked or partially cooked eggs should not be served to the very old, frail, young children, pregnant women or those with compromised immune systems.

First published in the United Kingdom in 2020 by Pavilion, 43 Great Ormond Street, London WC1N 3HZ

Copyright © Pavilion Books Company Ltd 2020
Text copyright © Ollie Hunter 2020
Photography copyright © Louise Hagger 2020

ISBN 978-1-91164-134-6

A CIP catalogue record for this book is available from the British Library.

10 9 8 7 6 5 4 3 2 1

Reproduction by Rival Colour Ltd, UK
Printed and bound by Leo Paper Products Ltd, China

www.pavilionbooks.com

MIX
Paper from responsible sources
FSC® C020056

Waterless Printing is applied on this product

30 Easy Ways to Join the FOOD Revolution

a sustainable cookbook

Ollie Hunter

PAVILION

CONTENTS

3

50% OF PRODUCE WITHIN 30 MILES

GETTING STARTED

WHAT IS SUSTAINABILITY?

- It's keeping the human species alive.
- It's creating a safe and beautiful place for our children.
- It's loving the resources that not only provide our food,
  but also our drinks, cars, phones, trainers or guitars.
- It means using new technology to help us reduce emissions.
- It's keeping the fish in our oceans alive for us to enjoy
  fish and chips.
- It's being more relaxed whilst cooking.
- It's quicker and cheaper.
- It's very social.
- It's creative.
- It's making your food taste so much better.
- It's listening to your body.
- It's feeling great whilst doing it.
- It's loving your body by loving the planet.
- It's the best diet for you and for the earth.

HOMO SAPIENS SAPIENS

Wow – what an extraordinary natural world we live in. A world where the largest organism is a mushroom 2400 acres large, the fastest animal is a peregrine falcon that can dive at speeds of up to 242 miles per hour, and there are roughly 10 times more stars in the sky than grains of sand in the world's deserts and beaches.

And at the same time, we humans have built our own forms of organism in the form of cities, far bigger than that mushroom, in planes we can fly 20 times faster than the falcon, and through science we have come to know about far more than just our immediate surroundings, but into space and beyond. We are an amazing species – we have achieved so much. Cured diseases, explored to the ends of the earth, created things that never existed on this planet before we made them; our intelligence is awe-inspiring.

And yet, we are completely dependent on everything we have conquered. Our wonderful ideas use nature's resources but are flawed in that they give nothing back in return. We are effectively abusing planet earth and taking advantage of our relationship with it. It's almost as if the doubling up of the words in our species name *homo sapiens sapiens* (man wise wise) has cancelled itself out. Are we really that wise if all that we have accomplished ultimately leads to our own destruction?

This book is not the complete guide to living sustainably, it is just the beginning. Part of the start of a beautiful period in time when, together, we will hopefully begin to solve the problems that we have created, so our wonderful species can continue to survive. And we can feel justified keeping the *sapiens* part of our species name.

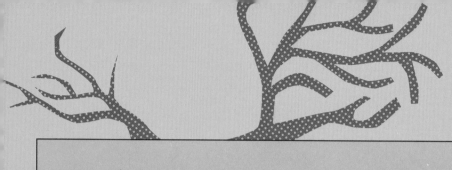

A FEW FACTS ABOUT THE WORLD TO MAKE US FEEL RUBBISH

- By 2050 there could be more plastic than fish in our oceans.
- 6.5 million people a year (not including animals) die from air pollution due to the burning of fossil fuels.
- One-third of greenhouse gases come from food production. A third of that alone comes from beef.
- A third of all agriculture comes from bee pollination, and yet the UK has lost 13 species of bees and a further 35 are facing extinction.
- Removal of forests accounts for 12–17% of greenhouse gases per year. All our rainforests could disappear in the next 100 years if we continue the same rate of deforestation.

- Water is used in excess – for every burger made, 3000 litres of water is used, which is equivalent to 4 years' worth of drinking water for one person.
- As a direct result of soil erosion, possibly 30% of the world's arable land has become unproductive in just 40 years.
- Treating obesity-related conditions is estimated to cost the NHS £5.1 billion a year in the UK.
- Insect biomass has reduced by 75% in the last 30 years.
- The world's 7.6 billion people represent just 0.01% of all living things, yet since the dawn of civilization, humanity has caused the loss of 83% of all wild mammals and half of all plants.

WHAT DOES THIS ACTUALLY MEAN?

- We may not be able to eat fish ever again – unless you want to eat plastic as well. I've heard it's a bit chewy.
- Our individual yearly food could cost about £3000 more each, because we might have to pollinate it ourselves. In fact, the first job for many of our children might even be a pollinator.
- We're finding it harder each year to produce enough food for our species. We may all have to eat rations.
- Unhealthy diets could be the tipping point as to whether the UK's free health service survives or not.
- Eating unsustainable beef is like filling your bedroom with methane.
- Deforestation is like filling your bedroom up with carbon dioxide.
- Eating unsustainable burgers is like drinking 3000 litres in 15 minutes.
- We as a species have contributed to more genocide than Hitler, Stalin and Chairman Mao combined.

IT'S NOT YOUR FAULT!

Let me start by saying, I'm sorry the world is in such a bad place – we know that there are problems and sustainability is one of the largest. The environment is changing faster than we can predict and it's scary.

But it's not fair that you should have all that pressure on your shoulders. Why should we have to individually burden ourselves with everything wrong in the world? We shouldn't. Life is difficult enough as it is, BUT the important thing is to understand why we have to make changes to our lifestyles. You can make a huge difference in the world just by doing small things – we all can. And what's more, we can have fun doing it.

We are all entitled to enjoy life, to have happiness, fulfilling relationships, support for our health, a good education, shelter and great food and drink. As long as our quest for the good life is sustainable, then life for future generations can also be wonderful and beautiful.

So... no more negativity about the end of the world, let's cook and eat delicious food to be sustainable.

Join the Sustainable Food Revolution.

#30food

ZERO

1 Grow Your Own

2 Stop Buying Plastic

3 Make Your Calories Count

4 The Road to Sustainable Eating

5

Root to
Fruit

7

Fish, Omega-3s
and Creativity

6

Thrifty
=
Delicious

To Meat or
Not to Meat

8

WASTE

GROW YOUR OWN

Today we're going to plant the seed of your journey to sustainability. You're joining the movement – congratulations! It's going be creative, it's going to be social, it's going to fun. And it's going to be delicious.

Now for an experiment – get ready to find out why we want to eat organic. You'll need to buy two plant pots, some compost, a packet of salad seeds and a bottle of pesticide. Fill up both pots with compost, and place them on your windowsill with a plate under each to catch the draining water. Follow the instructions on the packet to plant some seeds in each pot. Over the time you read this book,

whether it's a month or more, your seeds will grow. BUT you need to spray ONE plant with pesticides for the duration of its growth and leave the other organic. When the plants are big enough, taste leaves from both – that is if you want to after you've sprayed one – you'll find the organic tastes far better.

Salad leaves are one of the easiest things to grow, and each time you remove some leaves more will grow in their place! One of the best things about growing your own is it's great for the insects... we want lots more diversity! Growing your own also reduces the amount of packaging and food waste.

Spicy Seed Mix

Whilst we wait for our seeds to germinate and grow into salad, let's make something else using other seeds. This mix is great as a snack packed with goodness, or as a topping on salads, fish, meats and veg (page 14).

SERVES 4 AS A SNACK

500 G/1 LB 2 OZ MIXED SEEDS SUCH AS SUNFLOWER SEEDS, PUMPKIN SEEDS AND LINSEEDS, OR WHATEVER IS GROWN IN YOUR COUNTRY

1 TSP CHILLI FLAKES (HOT RED PEPPER FLAKES)

1 TBSP SMOKED PAPRIKA

1 TBSP GROUND CUMIN

½ TBSP SALT

OIL OF YOUR CHOICE, FOR DRIZZLING

Preheat the oven to 160°C fan/180°C/350°F/gas mark 4.

Mix all the ingredients together in a bowl and add just enough oil to coat the seeds. Spread out onto a baking sheet and bake for 10–15 minutes. Store in an airtight container for up to 4 weeks.

Dukkah

Dukkah is an amazing Egyptian spice blend that adds flavour to many dishes. Great on salads, meats, fish, roasted vegetables, flatbreads… the list goes on (page 15).

MAKES ENOUGH FOR 8 MEALS

50 G/1¾ OZ COBNUTS OR OTHER LOCALLY GROWN NUTS

2 TBSP SUNFLOWER SEEDS

1 TBSP FENNEL SEEDS

1 TBSP CUMIN SEEDS

1 TBSP CORIANDER SEEDS

1 TBSP POPPY SEEDS

1 TBSP BLACK ONION SEEDS

Preheat the oven to 140°C fan/160°C/325°F/gas mark 3.

Spread the cobnuts (or other nuts) and sunflower seeds on a baking sheet and bake for 10 minutes. Remove from the oven and leave to cool.

Place a decent frying pan (skillet) on the hob (stove top) over a medium heat. Toast the fennel seeds in the dry pan for 1 minute, then add to a large bowl. Toast the cumin seeds for a minute in the same pan, then add to the same bowl. Toast the coriander until they pop, then add to the bowl. Put the poppy seeds and black onion seeds into the bowl and, using the back of a rolling pin or a pestle and mortar, smash everything together to form a rough mix. Store for up to 3 months in an airtight jar or container.

STOP BUYING PLASTIC

I can't remember anyone telling me that it's okay to eat plastic. I don't fancy it either. But how about the poor fish that eat the plastic in our oceans? We're actually eating the fish that are eating the plastic. If you don't want to eat plastic, then we need to stop buying single-use plastic.

Three reasons to stop buying single-use plastic

1   You'll feel awesome about saving the oceans and our fish.

2   It's another step towards becoming a zero-waste legend.

3   There is no need to eat plastic, oil, detergent, pesticides or variations of mercury. I've heard they're not great for you!

ACTIONS TO TAKE

☐   Bring your own reusable shopping bags. If we all stop using single-use plastic bags, then supermarkets and grocery stores will stop providing them. We have the power to make this big change!

☐   Any vegetable that comes in plastic – don't buy it. Force the supermarkets to find another solution – they'll have to. Nature has its own protection, like cauliflower leaves, broad bean (fava bean) casings or hard squash skins.

☐   Go on holiday to somewhere by the sea, and spend a morning picking up litter off the beach.

☐   Buy a reusable water bottle – stainless steel is best, and you can generally use them for any drink you like.

☐   Buy toothpaste in glass containers.

☐   Visit shops with refill stations and bring your own containers to stock up on certain products and decrease the amount of packaging used.

☐   Visit a pick-your-own farm. They are a great day out and reduce waste and packaging.

☐   Shop at greengrocers and farmers' markets – they are always very good for quality produce and they normally wrap things in paper.

YOU EAT WHAT YOU WASTE

Single-use plastic is literally poisoning us. Here's why...

1
Plastic breaks down in the ocean into 'micro plastics'.

2
These absorb awful pollutants like oil, detergent, pesticides and mercury.

3
Tiny marine organisms eat these micro plastics – they're now in the animal food chain! Uh oh...

4
Very small fish eat the marine organisms. Then larger fish eat those fish. Then even larger fish eat those fish and so on... until you get to us.

4
We have now accumulated a high concentration of toxins in the fish we're eating.

5
Every time we pollute, we pollute the food chain that we are part of, polluting ourselves.

YOU HAVE THE FREE WILL TO FREE WILLY.

6
Change the way we waste, so we can change the way we eat.

Stop Buying Plastic

Pick Your Own Strawberries with Elderflower Panna Cottas

One for me, one for the basket? I'm only joking (I think). Picking your own fruit is such a great way to spend a sunny morning, and even though you haven't grown the produce yourself, you'll still feel like you've earned it. I think of this dish as a take on strawberries and cream, but in this case the cream is set into a delicious panna cotta flavoured with elderflower. It's a wonderful combination.

SERVES 4

350 ML/12 FL OZ/1½ CUPS DOUBLE CREAM (HEAVY CREAM)

150 ML/5 FL OZ/⅔ CUP WHOLE MILK

100 ML/3⅓ FL OZ/⅓ CUP ELDERFLOWER CORDIAL (PAGE 59)

2 TBSP CASTER (SUPERFINE) SUGAR

3 GELATINE LEAVES (GRASS FED OR VEGGIE)

1 TBSP FRESH LEMON JUICE

TO SERVE

200 G/7 OZ/2 CUPS FRESHLY PICKED STRAWBERRIES

30 G/1 OZ/2½ TBSP CASTER (SUPERFINE) SUGAR

EQUIPMENT

4 MOULDS OR RAMEKINS

Start by making the panna cottas. Stir together the cream, milk, elderflower cordial and sugar in a saucepan and bring to a simmer for a few minutes. Set aside.

Soak the gelatine leaves in cold water for 1 minute, then squeeze out the excess water and add to the warm cream mixture in the saucepan with the lemon juice. Stir well to make sure the gelatine is dissolved, then pour into moulds or ramekins. Place in the fridge for 6 hours to set.

Pick the green leaves off the strawberries (and put them in the compost), don't cut the leaves off the strawberries as it causes too much waste. Cut the berries in half and place in a bowl. Sprinkle the sugar over them and leave for 10 minutes to macerate. Because you've picked them yourself, they will taste at their very best, so you don't need a lot of sugar.

To serve, dip the bottom of each mould or ramekin into hot water for 30 seconds. You should then be able to turn them upside down for the panna cottas to easily slip out onto serving plates. If that hasn't happened, put back in the water for longer, then try again. Spoon the macerated strawberries over each panna cotta with some of the juices and serve.

Potato and Parsley Soup

Gazpacho

Despite their humble reputation, potatoes are incredibly diverse – Peru has over 4000 varieties alone – meaning you can enjoy the different flavours and textures each one has to offer. Here, they help to make this soup rich and creamy without the need for dairy. Try to buy, grow or borrow all the ingredients loose to make this soup totally plastic free!

Gazpacho is the raw definition of a summer garden – a perfectly balanced blend of sun-ripened vegetables. You can almost feel the warmth of the greenhouse and smell the tomatoes. Be sure to keep your vines to add them to the soup to enrich the flavour. Pick all the vegetables when they're at their best and ripest. Again, try and source all the ingredients here loose to avoid any plastic packaging.

SERVES 6

OIL OF YOUR CHOICE, FOR FRYING

2 ONIONS, ROUGHLY CHOPPED

6 GARLIC CLOVES, ROUGHLY CHOPPED

2 LEEKS (WHITES AND GREENS SEPARATED), CHOPPED

250 G/9 OZ POTATOES, PEELED AND ROUGHLY CHOPPED (MARFONA OR CAROLUS ARE GREAT ORGANIC VARIETIES)

1 BAY LEAF

100 G/3½ OZ/1 CUP FRESH PARSLEY STALKS, ROUGHLY CHOPPED (SAVE THE LEAVES FOR ANOTHER RECIPE)

SALT AND FRESHLY GROUND BLACK PEPPER

POACHED EGGS, TO SERVE (OPTIONAL)

SERVES 4

1 RED PEPPER

1 GREEN PEPPER

500 G/1 LB 2 OZ TOMATOES ON THE VINE

1 CUCUMBER

4 GARLIC CLOVES

2 TBSP RED WINE VINEGAR

SMALL HANDFUL OF FRESH BASIL

SMALL HANDFUL OF FRESH MARJORAM

SALT

100 ML/3⅓ FL OZ/⅓ CUP COLD-PRESSED OLIVE OIL, PLUS EXTRA TO SERVE

Put some glugs of oil in a large saucepan and place over a low–medium heat. Add the chopped onions, garlic and the leek whites to the pan and sauté until soft.

Add the peeled and chopped potatoes to the pan with about 2 litres/3½ pints/generous 8½ cups of cold water, the bay leaf and some salt and pepper. Bring to a simmer and cook for about 20 minutes until the potatoes are soft.

Add the leek greens and parsley stalks and simmer for 5 minutes. Remove the bay leaf and blitz the soup in a food processor until smooth. Warm through again before serving and top with a poached egg if you like.

This is super easy. Remove the stalks and seeds from the peppers and put in the compost. Remove the tomato vines and leave to one side. Put the peppers, tomatoes, cucumber, garlic cloves, vinegar, herbs, a pinch of salt and the olive oil in a food processor and blend. Pour into a container, add the tomato vines to infuse and chill completely for at least a couple of hours. You may need some extra vinegar or salt to taste.

To serve, just remove the tomato vines, ladle into bowls and drizzle with a little more cold-pressed oil.

MAKE YOUR CALORIES COUNT

'ENERGY CANNOT BE CREATED OR DESTROYED,
IT CAN ONLY BE CHANGED FROM ONE FORM
TO ANOTHER.'
– Einstein

Energy companies don't make energy, they take it from one source, change it and then send it to us for our TVs, phones or kettles, which we then use to make a hot cup of tea. We digest it and change it into another energy, and so on.

There are health problems, environmental problems, political problems and money problems that can all be fixed by changing energy in the right way.

Let's take an example. Imagine a beautiful farmer's field: it's growing delicious and nutritious potatoes. Farmer Spud is very happy with his produce. Well done, Spud.

Mr Crisp then comes along and buys all of Farmer Spud's potatoes. Very happy Farmer Spud.

Mr Crisp transports the potatoes to his factory where he processes them into crisps, packages them up with some extra nitrogen to preserve freshness and sends them to a distributor.

The distributor has lots of people working in an office (drinking lots of tea), trying to find buyers. The distributor sends crisps to shops.

Our shops are open all day ready for us to buy a packet of crisps. One of your friends is buying lunch and gets you a packet of cheese and onion. They bring it back to the office, but you hate cheese and onion flavour, so the crisps stay in the office until they are thrown away.

From a beautiful field of potatoes to the crisps being thrown away, a huge amount of energy is transferred and transformed. But here's the crucial bit: the energy is NOT being recycled back into making more crisps or fuel. Instead it's released as gas or heat, creating global warming. We need to reconnect the cycle!

So let's either cut out the middle people, who use more energy, and make crisps ourselves or let's get our crisp companies planting lots of trees to absorb the emissions.

By the way, I love crisps, I really do. But I don't eat crisps to survive. Let's make our calories count.

Parsnip Crisps

Flavoured Salts

Parsnips are one of those root vegetables that taste even better and sweeter after the first frost. The best method is to deep-fry these crisps for consistency and taste. You can use any root vegetable to make crisps in this way, including Farmer Spud's original potato.

MAKES AS MANY AS YOU WANT

2 PARSNIPS PER SERVING

OIL WITH A HIGH SMOKING POINT, SUCH AS RAPESEED OR SUNFLOWER, FOR DEEP-FRYING

SALT

Using a vegetable peeler, shave the parsnips into ribbons, skins as well. At a certain point it becomes hard to peel any more and you end up with just the middle part left – save these for roasting or for a soup or purée.

If you have an electric deep-fryer, turn it to 180°C/350°F. If you don't have one, then find a very deep heavy-bottomed pan and fill with 5 cm/2 inches of oil. Heat the oil to 180°C/350°F using a cooking thermometer, or until a cube of bread browns in 30 seconds. Deep-fry the parsnip ribbons until golden but not brown – every parsnip will fry at a different rate so keep a close eye on them rather than time them. Remove with a slotted spoon and drain any excess oil. Place in a bowl and sprinkle with a little salt before serving.

These are best eaten fresh and crisp but you can store leftovers in an airtight container for up to 1 week.

To cut down packaging, we now make our own crisps at the pub, no longer selling them in unsustainable bought-in foil packets. These flavoured salts are so easy to make and transform anything from the humble spud to a delicious risotto.

CHEESE AND ONION SALT

100 G/3½ OZ/GENEROUS 1 CUP GRATED CHEDDAR

100 G/3½ OZ/1⅔ CUPS FINELY DICED ONIONS

200 G/7 OZ/GENEROUS ¾ CUP SEA SALT

SPICY SALT

10 RED CHILLIES, THINLY SLICED

200 G/7 OZ/GENEROUS ¾ CUP SEA SALT

ROSEMARY SALT

100 G/3½ OZ FRESH ROSEMARY, FINELY CHOPPED

200 G/7 OZ/GENEROUS ¾ CUP SEA SALT

Preheat the oven to 90°C fan/110°C/225°F/gas mark ¼.

The simple method is the same for each of the variations above: mix all the ingredients for each recipe together thoroughly. Spread out well over a baking sheet and bake for about 2 hours. You want the mixture to come out bone dry. Leave to cool and then blend in a food processor until fine. Store in airtight containers for up to 6 months.

4

THE ROAD TO SUSTAINABLE EATING

Sustainability is creative. It's a bit like a mystery thriller that needs solving.

We've made a tasty meal, but now we have a problem – some leftovers or waste, so what do we do with it now? Don't throw it away, never throw it away, unless it didn't taste good the first time! Instead, let's come up with a way to reuse it. Take a foodie journey with me through making and reusing leftovers.

Shall we start with the staff of life? Bread. Freshly made bread is bloomin' marvellous and you've just made a great loaf. But after a few days it might be turning a little bit hard, so use it in a Tomato and Raspberry Salad (page 26) with rich ripe tomatoes – their juices will add moisture and flavour to the bread. Delicious. Another day goes by and the bread is a little harder – we definitely can't use it for morning toast, so let's use that crunch to our benefit and make croutons – I've chosen Summer Greens Minestrone Soup here (page 28), but it could be any stew or soup you want. Another day goes by, so slice the bread, then blitz it up into breadcrumbs. Breadcrumbs are great for topping pasta bakes, making veggie sausages, treacle tart and much more besides. The last resort is to add the bread to the compost bin, which will turn it back into soil to grow something else. Compost is so easy to keep, and you'll be rewarded with beautifully rich fertilizer, which you could always sell if you wanted. Or even make a wormery if you are feeling very experimental.

Bread

Tomato and Raspberry Salad

Summer Greens Minestrone Soup

Breadcrumbs

Compost

Why is this important?

Imagine if you spent all morning in the gym, sweated your heart out, and by 11am you're absolutely exhausted. But someone comes up to you and tells you that you didn't do it properly, so you only burnt half the number of calories you could have. Gutted? I would be. This is a bit like that. Nature and humans have spent all that time growing food to be eaten – to throw it away is inefficient and wasteful. It's like having to go to the gym twice as much to burn the same number of calories – we're all working much harder than we need to!

Wholemeal Loaf

There are definitely some moments when you can't beat white bread - a late night fish finger sandwich, a lazy Saturday morning French croissant and in bread and butter pudding after a Sunday roast. But for the rest of the time, a proper wholemeal loaf is a truly delicious and wholesome all-round option. It has a slightly nutty, even earthy flavour, with a pleasing natural sweetness. Whole grains contain more nutrients than white flour and when you use organic flour, you also avoid all those pesticide sprays that you don't want ending up on your plate. So let's underpin our sustainable journey by making the staff of life.

MAKES 1 LOAF

500 G/1 LB 2 OZ/GENEROUS 3¾ CUPS ORGANIC STRONG WHOLEMEAL (WHOLEWHEAT) BREAD FLOUR, PLUS EXTRA FOR THE WORK SURFACE

2 TBSP SALT

1 TBSP OLIVE OIL

15 G/½ OZ FRESH YEAST (OR 7 G/¼ OZ INSTANT DRIED YEAST)

320 ML/11 FL OZ/1⅓ CUPS TEPID WATER

EQUIPMENT
900-G/2-LB LOAF PAN

Mix together the flour, salt and olive oil in a mixing bowl. In a separate bowl, mix the yeast with the tepid water until dissolved using your hands, then mix into the flour. Bring the mixture together into a dough using your hands, then turn out onto a lightly floured work surface and knead for 10 minutes.

Put the dough back into the bowl, cover with a clean kitchen cloth and leave to prove in a warm area for an hour or until it has doubled in size.

Turn the dough out onto a lightly floured work surface and knock back by kneading through again for 5 minutes.

Shape the dough into a loaf, then transfer to the loaf pan. Leave to prove again in a warm place until it has risen to above the top of the pan.

Preheat the oven to 180°C fan/200°C/400°F/gas mark 6. Bake the loaf for 30–40 minutes until it sounds hollow when tapped. Remove from the oven and turn out onto a cooling rack.

Tomato and Raspberry Salad

This is a real taste of the English summer. Zingy, fresh, sweet, sour… and who doesn't like raspberries? I've always had a rhyming Spanish saying in my head *'mas color, mas sabor!'* which means more colour, more flavour! And it's so true in this dish. It goes amazingly well with barbecued red mullet, mackerel or lamb.

SERVES 2

4 SLICES SLIGHTLY STALE BREAD, CUT INTO SMALL CHUNKS

10 RIPE, JUICY PLUM TOMATOES, ROUGHLY CHOPPED

SMALL HANDFUL OF FRESH BASIL

SMALL HANDFUL OF FRESH MINT

SMALL HANDFUL OF FRESH MARJORAM

1 SMALL OR ½ LARGE RED ONION, FINELY DICED

LARGE HANDFUL OF FRESH RASPBERRIES

200 G/7 OZ RICOTTA OR MOZZARELLA CHEESE

FINE SALT

EDIBLE FLOWERS, TO GARNISH (OPTIONAL)

FOR THE DRESSING

50 ML/1⅔ FL OZ/3½ TBSP RED WINE OR CIDER VINEGAR, OR WHATEVER YOU HAVE TO HAND

1 TBSP RUNNY HONEY

200 ML/6¾ FL OZ/GENEROUS ¾ CUP DELICIOUS COLD-PRESSED OIL (I LOVE OLIVE OIL, BUT RAPESEED ALSO WORKS)

Add the chunks of slightly stale bread to a large mixing bowl. Add the chopped tomatoes, sprinkle them with a pinch of salt and leave for 15 minutes – this not only intensifies the flavour of the tomatoes but also draws out the liquid, which the bread will absorb.

Rip all the fresh herbs into pieces with your fingers and add to the bowl. Add the finely diced onion and the raspberries.

For the dressing, combine the vinegar, honey and oil in a small bowl and whisk together vigorously. Lightly drizzle some dressing over the salad.

Using your hands so as not to bruise the salad too much, mix the ingredients together, then mount the salad onto two serving plates. Scatter over your ricotta or mozzarella in blobs or chunks and finish with one last small drizzle of the dressing before serving. Garnish with edible flowers if you like.

Summer Greens Minestrone

This recipe is a great way to show off all the freshest vegetables in the middle of summer, plus it's full of fibre and vitamins. Because we're buying organic, you don't need to buy vegetable stock as the vegetables will have loads of flavour. I've never needed to add stock to any vegetable soup I've made. What you spend on organic veg you save by not having to buy vegetable stock.

SERVES 4

4 SLICES SLIGHTLY STALE BREAD, CUT INTO CHUNKS

COLD-PRESSED OLIVE OIL, FOR FRYING AND DRIZZLING

2 ONIONS, FINELY DICED

6 GARLIC CLOVES, FINELY DICED

2 LEEKS, FINELY DICED

1 FENNEL BULB, FINELY DICED

80 G/3 OZ DRIED SPAGHETTI, BROKEN UP INTO SMALL PIECES

4 COURGETTES (ZUCCHINI), SLICED

LARGE HANDFUL OF FRESH PEAS

LARGE HANDFUL OF BROAD BEANS (FAVA BEANS)

LARGE HANDFUL OF MIXED FRESH MINT, PARSLEY AND BASIL, ROUGHLY CHOPPED

SALT

Preheat the oven to 180°C fan/200°C/400°F/gas mark 6.

First, make the croutons. Space the chunks of slightly stale bread out on a baking sheet and drizzle with oil. Roast in the oven for 10 minutes, then set to one side to cool while you make the soup.

Glug some olive oil into a saucepan and place over a low–medium heat. Add the finely diced onions, garlic, leeks and fennel and sauté until soft.

Add 1 litre/1¾ pints/4 cups of cold water to the pan, bring to the boil and then add the spaghetti. Simmer for 7 minutes, then add the courgettes, peas and broad beans and cook for another 3 minutes. Season the soup with salt and mix in the herbs. Ladle into bowls and serve with a drizzle of olive oil and the croutons scattered into the soup.

ROOT TO FRUIT

Root to fruit is the same theory as nose to tail, an ethos made great by Fergus Henderson, a hero in the chef world. The only difference is that we're now focusing on vegetables and fruits. It's a bit like using the cheaper cuts from an animal, like lamb shoulder or beef shin, and turning them into something wonderful.

Carrot tops, broad bean (fava bean) casings, celeriac leaves and beetroot stalks – these are all decent foods that we can eat.

If you think about it, supermarkets are only selling us half the vegetable, so they're actually ripping us off! If you buy a carrot, it should come with the green top. It's like buying some running trainers without the laces – you wouldn't stand for that.

All of the below are full of flavour, minerals and loads of nutrients. You can add them to soups, make salads, smoothies or stir-fries with them. Be aware that there are vegetable or fruit leaves, like rhubarb, tomato and potato, that are poisonous – don't eat these. If in doubt always seek advice first before you eat.

Squash seeds Fried in oil and sprinkled with salt, they make a great snack

Carrot tops Great for pesto, stir-fry, chicken with carrot mash and carrot top greens

Beetroot leaves Use in curries or salads

Turnip greens Good in stews, pies or curries

Courgette (zucchini) stalks Cut into penne pasta shapes and cook like pasta

Broccoli stalks Use in soup, stir-fry or coleslaw

Broad bean (fava bean) casings Make delicious soups or creams

Pea shoots Make a beautiful garnish or salad

Herb stalks Finely chop and use like onion in sauces, in flavoured oils or vinegars and in salads

Root veg skins I never peel my veg because I use organic, but the peelings make great crisps

Brussels sprout tops For greens, salads, curry or even smoothies

Celeriac tops Use instead of celery

Fennel tops Great for flavoured oils, vinegars, salads or dressings

Beetroot Leaf Dhal

One of the great things about eating from root to fruit is the added variety of flavours and textures available to us. For example, sage flowers have the subtle taste of sage but are a little more floral than the leaves. Pea shoots offer a lighter and more delicate pea flavour than the pea. In this recipe, beetroot stalks bring that earthy beetroot taste, but with added crunch and freshness.

SERVES 2

100 G/3½ OZ/½ CUP DRIED RED SPLIT LENTILS OR SPLIT PEAS

OIL WITH A HIGH SMOKING POINT SUCH AS RAPESEED OR SUNFLOWER, FOR FRYING

1 ONION, DICED

CHUNK OF FRESH GINGER, DICED

6 GARLIC CLOVES, DICED

HANDFUL OF FRESH CORIANDER (CILANTRO), STALKS DICED AND LEAVES LEFT WHOLE

1 RED CHILLI, DICED

1 CINNAMON STICK

1 TSP GROUND CUMIN

1 TSP GROUND CORIANDER

1 TSP GROUND TURMERIC

1 TSP BLACK MUSTARD SEEDS

4 FRESH TOMATOES, CHOPPED (OR ½ X 400-G/14-OZ CAN OF TOMATOES)

4 BEETROOT STALKS AND LEAVES, THINLY SLICED (SAVE THE BEETROOT FOR ANOTHER MEAL)

SALT

DOLLOPS OF PLAIN YOGURT, TO SERVE

If you're using split peas, then they'll need to be soaked overnight in plenty of cold water before using.

Put a good amount of oil into a large pan (skillet) over a medium–high heat. Add the diced onion, ginger, garlic, coriander stalks and chilli and fry until soft.

Once they're soft, add the cinnamon stick, ground spices, mustard seeds and continue to cook for 2 minutes, stirring occasionally. Add the tomatoes and lentils or soaked and drained split peas. Season to taste with salt and stir. Add 1 litre/1¾ pints/4 cups of cold water. Bring to a simmer and cook for 15 minutes if using lentils or 40 minutes if using split peas.

Stir in the sliced beetroot stalks and leaves for the final 5 minutes of cooking. Serve the dhal scattered with the fresh coriander leaves and dollops of yogurt.

Carrot Top Stir-Fry

Carrots are usually sold to us without their tops on in supermarkets, which, to be honest, is a little cheeky as it is only about half the crop. So in theory we could all be spending less on our weekly shop if supermarkets included them! Carrot tops taste a little bit like how carrots smell - slightly earthy, fresh and distinctly carroty. When buying, look for younger greens that are softer and easier to eat and have fun experimenting with using them in different ways. They are good in stews, pestos, vegetable soups or stir-fries like this one.

SERVES 2

2 TBSP SESAME OIL

2 TBSP RAPESEED OIL

1 ONION, FINELY DICED

6 GARLIC CLOVES, FINELY DICED

CHUNK OF FRESH GINGER, FINELY DICED

1 RED CHILLI, FINELY DICED

BUNCH OF FRESH CORIANDER (CILANTRO), STALKS DICED AND LEAVES LEFT WHOLE, PLUS EXTRA TO GARNISH

1 TSP CHINESE FIVE-SPICE POWDER

1 SPRING ONION (SCALLION), SLICED

4 CARROTS WITH THEIR TOPS, BOTH FINELY CHOPPED

FEW DASHES OF WORCESTERSHIRE SAUCE (PAGE 84) OR MUSHROOM KETCHUP (PAGE 64)

1 TBSP HONEY

JUICE OF ½ LIME

HANDFUL OF NUTS OF YOUR CHOICE

2 TBSP SESAME SEEDS

Put the sesame oil and rapeseed oil into a large frying pan (skillet) or wok over a medium heat. Add the finely diced onion, garlic, ginger, chilli and coriander stalks and stir-fry until just soft.

Add the Chinese five-spice, chopped spring onion and the carrots plus their tops. Stir-fry over a high heat until the carrots are soft enough for your liking. Stir in the Worcestershire Sauce or Mushroom Ketchup, honey, lime juice, nuts, coriander leaves and sesame seeds to finish. Serve with more fresh coriander on top.

THRIFTY :
DELICIOUS

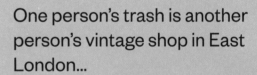

One person's trash is another person's vintage shop in East London...

Kale was a weed until 10 years ago, and oysters used to be eaten with a pint of ale in pubs rather than with champagne in airport lounges.

Being thrifty isn't about returning to wartime routines, it's about being savvy. Using all the odds and ends, the nooks and crannies, the woody and the tough, the gnarly, the gristly. And by cooking them properly, you can make something delicious and very cheap. It's a bit like finding all the best vinyls in your parents' garage.

Asparagus Ends Soup

This is sustainability at its best. Asparagus is a wonderful, delicious and highly seasonal vegetable. It comes and goes like a New Year's resolution, but unlike the former it is far more anticipated and appreciated. When prepping asparagus, a good trick is to gently snap off the stem near the base - this natural break is a sign to remove the woody ends which are normally inedible, however this recipe turns them into something sweet and scrummy.

SERVES 4

OIL, FOR FRYING

2 ONIONS, ROUGHLY CHOPPED

6 GARLIC CLOVES, ROUGHLY CHOPPED

100 ML/3⅓ FL OZ/⅓ CUP WHITE WINE OR 3 TBSP VINEGAR OF YOUR CHOICE

600 G/21 OZ ASPARAGUS ENDS

300 ML/10 FL OZ/1¼ CUPS DOUBLE (HEAVY) CREAM (OR A DAIRY-FREE ALTERNATIVE OF YOUR CHOICE)

TO SERVE (OPTIONAL)

COLD-PRESSED OIL OF YOUR CHOICE

ASPARAGUS LEAVES OR MUSTARD LEAVES AND/OR CHIVE FLOWERS

Put a couple of glugs of oil into a large saucepan over a medium heat and sauté the chopped onions and garlic until soft. Add the wine or vinegar and let bubble for a couple of minutes to reduce.

Pour in 500 ml/17 fl oz/2 cups of cold water, then turn the heat up and bring to a rapid boil for a few minutes. Add the asparagus ends and cook for 2 minutes or until they turn vibrant green. Add the cream and simmer for 2 more minutes. Immediately take off the heat and blitz the soup in a food processor or using a stick blender until smooth.

Pass through a sieve (strainer) and you'll have a beautiful asparagus cream. Here we've warmed it through and served it as a soup topped with cold-pressed oil, asparagus leaves and chive flowers. Alternatively, you can reduce the asparagus cream further in a pan and use as a delicious pasta sauce.

TIP

Exactly the same recipe can be made using broad bean (fava bean) casings instead of asparagus ends. These beans come with a protective outer casing, which has a lining soft enough to be a baby's blanket. People generally remove these cases and throw them away, but they have loads of flavour and are effectively a bonus free ingredient.

Thrifty = Delicious

Homemade Limoncello

Lemon Cordial

This is a great way to use up the peel on lemons you have bought for adding juice to other dishes. So every time you're making a lemon dressing or a vodka and tonic, peel the lemons first and add the peelings with the pith removed to the jar of alcohol. Organic lemons are always best, one reason being because the rinds are unwaxed and more suitable for consuming.

Another easy and delicious way to use up leftover lemon peel: for this cordial you need to collect and store the peelings in sugar. Nothing wasted makes life taste better.

MAKES 1 LITRE/ 1¾ PINT

700 ML/1½ PINTS/3 CUPS VODKA OR ANOTHER PLAIN SPIRIT

250 G/9 OZ/1¼ CUPS CASTER (SUPERFINE) SUGAR

LOTS OF LEFTOVER LEMON PEEL (THE MORE THE BETTER)

EQUIPMENT

1 LITRE/ 1¾ PINT STERILIZED MASON/KILNER JAR OR GLASS BOTTLE

Place the vodka or other spirit into the glass jar or bottle and add the sugar. Shake to dissolve the sugar. Now you can start adding your flavourings. Over time, add your leftover lemon peelings to the jar or bottle, replace the lid and give it a quick shake to combine.

Depending on how many lemons you use, the limoncello should be ready for tasting after a month or two. Serve chilled for sipping in shot glasses.

MAKES 1 LITRE/ 1¾ PINT

500 G/18 OZ/2½ CUPS CASTER (SUPERFINE) SUGAR

LOTS OF LEFTOVER LEMON PEEL (YOU'LL NEED AT LEAST 12 LEMONS WORTH)

EQUIPMENT

1 LITRE/ 1¾ PINT STERILIZED MASON/KILNER JAR OR GLASS BOTTLE

Place the sugar in a large container with a lid. As you collect your leftover lemon peel, store it in the container of sugar, pushing the peelings down until they are nicely submerged and replacing the lid.

Once you have enough peel collected, add the sugar and peelings to a saucepan with 500 ml/17 fl oz/2 cups water. Boil for 5 minutes. Blitz in a food processor and then strain and let cool. Bottle the cordial and store in the fridge for 3–6 months.

TIP

You can make liqueurs in the same way as the limoncello with any other produce you have in abundance. Try a strawberry one with a glut of strawberries, or maybe a minty one if you have a flourishing mint plant.

7

FISH, OMEGA-3S AND CREATIVITY

There is the most fantastic book called *The Madness of Adam and Eve* by David Horrobin. Within it, he starts by arguing that there was a pivotal moment when we changed from ancient apes, *homo sapiens*, to *homo sapiens sapiens*, and the reason was because of our intake of fish and other water-based organisms. Basically, the magical omega-3 fats. He argues that our intake of these fats led to the beginnings of creativity, which allowed us to evolve far quicker than other species.

Horrobin then goes on to theorize about the link between creative geniuses like Van Gogh, Einstein and Michaelangelo and increased instances of schizophrenia, psychopathy and mania, which is an interesting idea. But the foundation of his theory, of the amazing benefits of omega-3 fatty acids, is the part that has the strong scientific proof to back it up which has led our species to increased creativity, curiosity and ambition.

OMEGA-3S

We can get a huge amount of these, especially EPA and DHA, from oily fish. ALA, another omega-3 fatty acid, is found in plant-based sources such as nuts and seeds, but here we're going to focus on fish. The NHS recommends eating one portion of oily fish a week just for the omega-3s. There are many studies that show the wonderful positive affects of omega-3s on our brain performance. Learn where they come from and eat them sustainably, as generally the more sustainable the source, the richer the omega-3s present:

- Anchovies
- Sardines
- Herring
- Mackerel
- Trout
- Mussels
- Squid
- Crab
- Fish oil
- Seaweed... not a fish, but we're going straight to the source!

Red Dulse Carbonara

Red dulse is a type of seaweed that is rich in health benefits, including those all-important omega-3s. It has a satisfying, savoury taste and subtle bacon flavour that works perfectly in carbonara in place of the usual meat. Organic eggs are also rich in omega-3s so this dish is a double whammy. I like to use good-quality bronze die cut spaghetti, which has a rough texture that the sauce loves to stick to. It might be a little more expensive but it's worth it.

SERVES 4

360 G/12½ OZ DRIED BRONZE DIE CUT SPAGHETTI

EXTRA VIRGIN OLIVE OIL, FOR FRYING, PLUS EXTRA TO SERVE

8 TBSP DULSE FLAKES

4 GARLIC CLOVES, THINLY SLICED

200 ML/6¾ FL OZ/GENEROUS ¾ CUP WHITE WINE

200 G/7 OZ/SCANT 1 CUP DOUBLE (HEAVY) CREAM

BUNCH OF FRESH PARSLEY, ROUGHLY CHOPPED

4 EGG YOLKS

SALT

Bring a pan of salted water to the boil. Add the spaghetti and cook until al dente, which should take roughly 8–10 minutes (check the instructions on your packet).

Meanwhile, put a couple of glugs of extra virgin olive oil in a saucepan over a low–medium heat and sauté the dulse flakes for 2 minutes until soft. Add the sliced garlic and sauté for a further minute. Add the white wine and cook out for a couple of minutes until the wine has reduced by half, then stir in the cream and heat through.

Drain the cooked spaghetti, reserving 2 tablespoons of the cooking water, and add both to the dulse sauce in the pan. Using tongs, stir the pasta with the sauce, making sure each piece is fully coated.

Remove the pan from the heat and chuck in the parsley and season with salt. At this point you can either add the egg yolks to the pasta to finish the sauce in the pan or leave them to one side to garnish each plate individually. If you've added the yolks to the pan, stir well again and let the sauce thicken in the residual heat for a minute or two.

Serve the pasta drizzled with more delicious extra virgin olive oil. If you've reserved the egg yolks, top each bowl of hot pasta with a yolk and let your guests swirl them into their own plate before eating.

Curried Mussels

Rope-grown mussels are one of the most sustainable sources of omega-3s and 100 g/3½ oz of mussels represents 23% of your recommended weekly intake of omega-3. Serve this dish with crusty bread to mop up the umami, salty juices.

SERVES 2 AS A MAIN OR 4 AS AN APPETIZER

OIL, FOR FRYING

1 ONION, FINELY CHOPPED

3 GARLIC CLOVES, FINELY CHOPPED

1 RED CHILLI, FINELY CHOPPED

CHUNK OF FRESH GINGER, FINELY CHOPPED

BUNCH OF FRESH CORIANDER (CILANTRO), STALKS FINELY CHOPPED AND LEAVES LEFT WHOLE

1 TSP GROUND CORIANDER

1 TSP GROUND TURMERIC

1 X 400-ML/14-FL OZ CAN OF COCONUT MILK

1 KG/2 LB 4 OZ DEEP SEA ROPE-GROWN MUSSELS, CLEANED IF NEEDED

1 LIME

CRUSTY BREAD, TO SERVE

Put the oil into a large saucepan over a medium heat. Add the finely chopped onion, garlic, chilli, ginger and coriander stalks and sauté until soft.

Stir in the ground coriander and turmeric and cook for 2 more minutes. Add the coconut milk and bring to a simmer. When simmering, add all the mussels and cover the pan with a lid. Cook for 3–5 minutes, until all the mussels have properly opened. Discard any that haven't opened after this time.

Divide the steaming mussels and sauce between serving bowls. Cut the lime into wedges and squeeze over each bowl. Scatter with fresh coriander leaves and serve with crusty bread.

South of France Fish Soup

Fish bones can produce one of the most delicious meals ever. You may need a glass of rosé and a table in the south of France, but if those aren't to hand then this dish can transport you there instead. Fish bones are free and every fishmonger will have them.

SERVES 8

OLIVE OIL, FOR FRYING

2 ONIONS, ROUGHLY CHOPPED

1 LEEK, ROUGHLY CHOPPED

1 FENNEL BULB, ROUGHLY CHOPPED

6 GARLIC CLOVES, ROUGHLY CHOPPED

PINCH OF SAFFRON THREADS

200 ML/6¾ FL OZ/GENEROUS ¾ CUP HOT WATER

1 STAR ANISE

3 BAY LEAVES

1 TBSP FENNEL SEEDS

500 G/1 LB 2 OZ FRESH TOMATOES OR 1 X 400-G/14-OZ CAN OF TOMATOES

1 KG/2 LB 4 OZ FISH BONES - FROM A RED FISH LIKE MULLET, OR GURNARD AND SEA BASS ARE ALSO GREAT

3 LARGE STRIPS OF ORANGE PEEL FROM 1 ORANGE

BUNCH OF FRESH BASIL

TO SERVE

AIOLI

CROUTONS

GRATED MILD HARD CHEESE

Put some olive oil into a saucepan over a medium heat. Add the chopped onions, leek, fennel and garlic and sauté until soft.

Place the saffron threads in a bowl, pour the hot water over them and set to one side... this will get the aromas going. Now add the star anise, bay leaves and fennel seeds to the saucepan and cook for a few minutes before adding the tomatoes, saffron water and fish bones. Top up the pan with more water to cover the bones, add the orange peel, bring up the heat and simmer for 1 hour.

After your patient wait, remove the star anise and add the fresh basil. Blitz the soup in a food processor – bones and all – in batches if needed. Take care to not overfill the processor, and to be safe, place a kitchen towel over the lid, to help catch anything that does spill out.

Strain the soup through a sieve (strainer). Heat through again to serve. Delicious with aioli, croutons and some grated mild hard cheese.

TO MEAT OR NOT TO MEAT

There is so much debate on this subject. But why on earth did humans eat meat in the first place?

We ate it to survive! Surely everyone knows this... it was logical and intentional. We also survived off other animal products like dairy, eggs, manure for soil richness and leather for clothes. We ate meat because it tastes good, and it tastes good because our bodies know it is a highly dense source of protein and nutrients with some healthy fats. In the previous chapter we talked about oily fish and omega-3s, but grass-fed animals also have them. We trusted our bodies before there was science. Eating meat meant we could spend less time farming and eating, and more time evolving and creating civilization. Finally, we ate meat as a way of bringing the family or community together to celebrate the week, as we still do with the English Sunday roast or a summer barbecue (grill party).

So how has meat changed? Cows went from eating only grass to eating commercially produced grain all year round – animals like cows, deer, sheep and even pigs evolved to eat grass, which means their meat contains omega-3s too – the magical nutrients that are great for us and our brains. BUT the concentration is found most in grass-fed animals. And this goes for milk and dairy too.

Now we have such an abundance of food, do we really need to eat meat to survive? Probably not. Do we need to eat animals for nutrients – maybe, but we need oily fish the most. Do we still need to eat meat to evolve? Probably not. Do we need food to bring us together – yes and it's really good at doing it, but again maybe not meat.

Food evolves, diets change, desires wander, and over hundreds of years we find that we have moved completely away from the reason we ever started doing something. At what point do we ask – have we taken this too far?

The conclusion

I'm afraid it is now a fact that we all need to reduce the amount of meat we are eating, both for our health and the health of the world. Red meat is very much one of the worst contributors to our problems and this should be reduced to almost 1% of our diet. It's not necessarily the consumption of meat per se, but the consumption of all the food and water the cow has to have before we eat it – this is the major reason that eating meat regularly is unsustainable.

So, let's eat less but better quality meat, making sure it has been respected, like any other organism on this planet, and that it is organic and grass-fed where possible. Our beautiful and symbiotic relationship with animals continues to evolve, hopefully to better their lives.

Veggie meat

There are many dishes that don't rely on meat for their flavour. So, what plant-based ingredients can we replace the meat with? At the pub we keep an abundance of great vegetables and dry stores to use instead of meat – and our customers love our alternatives like lentil Bolognese, bean, walnut and squash burger with spicy mayo, aubergine (eggplant) parmigiana with Cheddar and mushroom Wellington with chestnuts.

What do we crave most with meat? Fat, protein and salt. If you can imitate these flavours in veggie food, then you can create some amazing meals. Vegetables are so much more diverse in flavour – especially if you apply techniques like caramelizing to extract the most amount of salt, sweetness and flavour.

Nose to tail ethos

A sustainable way to eat meat is to buy whole animals. For example, ask your butcher if you and a few mates can buy a whole organic lamb, then split the meat and freeze it – it'll save you money in the long run. A whole organic chicken in the UK costs roughly £12, and from this I'll show you how to make three meals for two people, so it works out as roughly £1.50 per person! You could also even take the tenderloins from the breast to make chicken nuggets and use the livers in an appetizer, which would make it even more economical.

Juan pot dishes

Growing up, our family used to give the 'one pot' dish a pseudonym – it was otherwise know as a 'juan pot'. Some sort of Spanish machismo with big, bold, punchy flavours. This is one of the best ways to cook sustainably because you have so little washing up to do! Cutting down on water is not only great for your bank balance, but also uses less water and less energy.

On the following few pages, I'm going to give you three amazing recipes to make three dishes from one purchase – a whole chicken.

First, remove the chicken breasts and leave in your fridge for another day, these are for the tagine (page 46). You can always ask your butcher to do this for you. Next, roast the chicken whole for about 45 minutes in an oven set to 180°C fan/200°C/400°F/gas mark 6. Strip the cooked meat from the chicken and set aside for the pie (page 49).

Now make a stock. Add the chicken carcass to your largest saucepan. Throw in some vegetables like leeks, onion, garlic and herb stalks, cover with water and simmer for 1–2 hours. Strain into airtight containers and store in the fridge for up to 2 weeks or in the freezer for up to 6 months. We will use the stock in a risotto (see right).

THE EMOTIONAL SIDE OF MEAT

This subject is a little less obvious to everyone. Some people think animals have emotions, some don't. Some people think vegetables have feelings, some don't. Some people think their partners are emotionally non-existent, some don't. No matter what your beliefs or thoughts, there is no denying that humans create relationships with animals. Animals are non-judgemental, they help us, they can give us positive energy and they can make us happy. And as a result, most of us find it hard, very hard, to kill them.

If we had to survive, I would imagine most people would or could kill in the end. However, it's not something we want to do. But we do like to eat meat.

So, we camouflage the killing process by giving it a French name, the abattoir, which means to 'beat down', from the French *abattre*. Like many unpleasant things, we hide the truth behind another name – a pig is now pork, a cow is now beef and a baby cow is veal. So yes, killing is the hardest part, but by giving it to someone else to do we release ourselves from the emotional trauma and we eat meat with no guilt.

There is nothing in the education system that teaches our children about where food comes from. Usually, children have no idea of where their meat comes from, or even of the concept that meat is an animal that has been killed for us. This provides no basis for them to be able to comprehend the more emotionally complex notion that humans are also animals. To me this begs the question: to what extent are we using nature, not only to survive, but to eat greedily for our own pleasure by ignoring the emotionally crippling idea of mass genocide that creates huge profits but is damaging to the resources of our planet?

If you're happy that your demand to eat meat means that animals are killed, then emotionally you must be okay with it. I have had to kill animals before – it's pretty rubbish. But I know where it has come from, appreciate it in its entirety and now, as a result, I rarely eat it. Whether I'll eat meat in 10 years' time, I don't know. It's an ever-changing mindset for me and that's okay.

Side note – as soon as my wife and I got a dog, I immediately changed my perception of animals. I had a very strong relationship with him and, on my commute to work, all I could see in a field of lambs was lots of copies of our dog. I emotionally put my relationship with our dog into all animals. It brought me closer to the natural world and further away from the idea of wanting to kill an animal to eat meat.

Chicken Stock and Mushroom Risotto with Nasturtiums

Mushroom risotto conjures up awful memories as it's been overused and under-flavoured for too many years. Let's celebrate it properly by using some local grains and other good-quality ingredients. The secret to this is the chicken stock, which you've already made! The rest is easy.

SERVES 2

OLIVE OIL, FOR FRYING, PLUS GOOD-QUALITY OLIVE OIL TO SERVE

1 ONION, FINELY DICED

6 GARLIC CLOVES, FINELY DICED

1 LEEK, FINELY DICED

BUNCH OF FRESH PARSLEY, STALKS FINELY DICED AND LEAVES CHOPPED

SMALL BUNCH OF FRESH THYME, LEAVES PICKED AND FINELY DICED

250 G/9 OZ MUSHROOMS, SLICED

150 G/5½ OZ/SCANT 1 CUP DRIED SPELT GRAINS

100 ML/3⅓ FL OZ/⅓ CUP WHITE WINE, CIDER (HARD CIDER) OR WATER

500 ML/17 FL OZ/2 CUPS FRESH CHICKEN STOCK (SEE LEFT)

NASTURTIUM LEAVES, PLUS FLOWERS, TO GARNISH

SALT

LOCALLY SOURCED HARD CHEESE, FOR GRATING OVER

Put some glugs of olive oil in a large saucepan over a low–medium heat. Add the diced onion, garlic, leek, parsley stalks and thyme leaves and sauté until soft. Add the sliced mushrooms and continue to cook for 10–15 minutes to caramelize the mushrooms. Add the spelt, the wine, cider or water and season with salt.

Now turn the heat down low and slowly add the chicken stock (adding it cold is fine), ladle by ladle, over 40 minutes to slowly cook the grains. Keep cooking until the spelt is tender; you can add more water or stock if you need.

Finish by stirring in the chopped parsley leaves, the nasturtium leaves and any last-minute seasoning. Serve topped with grated hard cheese, nasturtium flowers and drizzles of good-quality olive oil.

Chicken Breast Tagine with Locally Dried Fruit

Use the chicken breasts in this spicy, warming one-pan dish, along with locally grown dried fruits. My mum has a prolific damson tree that produces plump fruit, perfect for drying and storing for this very recipe. If you grow a tree it'll keep giving back, year after year, a bit like an abundantly generous godmother.

SERVES 2

1 TBSP GROUND CUMIN

1 TBSP GROUND CORIANDER

1 TBSP GROUND TURMERIC

1 TBSP PAPRIKA

2 RAW CHICKEN BREASTS FROM OUR WHOLE CHICKEN

OIL OF YOUR CHOICE, FOR FRYING

1 ONION, DICED

6 GARLIC CLOVES, DICED

HANDFUL OF FRESH CORIANDER (CILANTRO), STALKS DICED AND LEAVES LEFT WHOLE

1 RED CHILLI, DICED

100 ML/3⅓ FL OZ/⅓ CUP RED WINE, WATER OR EVEN CIDER (HARD CIDER)

1 X 400-G/14-OZ CAN CHOPPED TOMATOES

1 TBSP APPLE MOLASSES, OR USE WHATEVER MOLASSES IS LOCALLY PRODUCED

1 X 400-G/14-OZ COOKED BEANS OR PULSES – CANNELLINI BEANS ARE DELICIOUS

HANDFUL OF LOCAL DRIED FRUITS SUCH AS PRUNES, DAMSONS OR APRICOTS, PITTED

SALT

TO SERVE

DOLLOPS OF PLAIN YOGURT

GRAINS SUCH AS SPELT OR COUSCOUS, COOKED

Preheat the oven to 180°C fan/200°C/400°F/gas mark 6.

Mix all the spices together and set aside. Rub the chicken breasts with 1 tbsp of the spice mix. Add a few glugs of oil to an ovenproof saucepan and place over a medium heat. Quickly fry the chicken breasts just to sear the outside on both sides, then remove from the pan and leave to one side.

Add some more oil to the same pan and then sauté the diced onion, garlic, coriander stalks and chilli until soft. Once soft, stir in the rest of the spice mix and cook for a few minutes. Add the wine, cider or water to deglaze the pan. Add the tomatoes and molasses and give it a little stir. Simmer for 10 minutes to reduce the sauce.

Add the drained beans or pulses and dried fruit, stir and season with salt. Nestle each seared chicken breast into the sauce, then add 100 ml/3⅓ fl oz/⅓ cup cold water and transfer to the oven to cook for 30–35 minutes.

Serve the tagine scattered with fresh coriander leaves and perhaps some edible flowers, with dollops of yogurt and some spelt or couscous.

Chicken Leg, Blue Cheese and Nettle Pie

Choose an ovenproof saucepan for this dish and you'll have minimal washing up! Serve with lots of steamed vegetables on the side.

SERVES 2–3

FOR THE PASTRY

120 G/4¼ OZ/1 CUP MINUS 1½ TBSP PLAIN (ALL-PURPOSE) FLOUR, PLUS EXTRA FOR THE WORK SURFACE

60 G/2 OZ/½ STICK COLD SALTED BUTTER, CUBED

1–2 TBSP COLD WATER

PINCH OF SALT

1 EGG, BEATEN, FOR BRUSHING

FOR THE FILLING

OIL, FOR FRYING

2 ONIONS, FINELY CHOPPED

6 GARLIC CLOVES, FINELY CHOPPED

BUNCH OF FRESH PARSLEY, STALKS AND LEAVES SEPARATED, BOTH FINELY CHOPPED

SMALL BUNCH OF FRESH THYME, LEAVES PICKED AND CHOPPED

2 LEEKS, SLICED

75 G/2⅔ OZ/¾ STICK SALTED BUTTER

50 G/1¾ OZ/GENEROUS ⅓ CUP PLAIN (ALL-PURPOSE) FLOUR

250 ML/8½ FL OZ/1 CUP MILK OR STOCK

COOKED LEG MEAT FROM 1 CHICKEN

1 TBSP MUSTARD

SALT

VERY LARGE HANDFUL FRESH NETTLES, LEAVES PICKED WEARING GLOVES, PLUS EXTRA TO GARNISH (OPTIONAL)

80 G/3 OZ LOCAL BLUE CHEESE, CUBED

Preheat the oven to 200°C fan/220°C/425°F/gas mark 7.

Start by making the pastry, which doesn't take long at all... put the flour, butter, cold water and a pinch of salt in a large mixing bowl. Using your fingertips and working quickly, rub the cubed butter into the flour until it becomes the texture of coarse breadcrumbs. Now bring the dough together into a smooth ball with your hands, kneading a little and adding a dash more cold water if needed. Lightly flour a work surface and use a rolling pin to roll the pastry out into a circle, roughly the same size as your pan and about 2.5 cm/½ inch thick. Carefully transfer the pastry to a plate, cover with a kitchen towel and leave in the fridge while you make the filling.

Put a few glugs of oil into a large ovenproof saucepan over a medium heat. Add the chopped onions, garlic, parsley stalks and thyme and sauté until soft. Add the sliced leeks and continue cooking for 5 minutes until soft.

Add the butter and let it melt. Add the flour and stir around all the vegetables to let it cook out for 5 minutes. Now slowly add the milk (or stock), little by little, stirring with each addition until it's combined into a smooth sauce surrounded by vegetables. Add the cooked chicken leg meat, mustard, a pinch of salt, chopped parsley leaves and nettle leaves to the sauce. Add the blue cheese and give the sauce a final stir. Heat through until the cheese is melted and combined and then turn off the heat.

Take the pastry out of the fridge and layer it on top of the sauce, pushing it down slightly around the edges. Brush the pastry with the beaten egg then bake for 35–40 minutes until the pastry is golden. If you want to decorate the pie top with extra nettles they will need to be cooked, so 5 minutes before the end of cooking time remove the pie, place the nettles on top and brush with a little more egg wash before baking for the final 5 minutes. Serve.

ORGANIC

SEASONAL

CAULIFLOWER

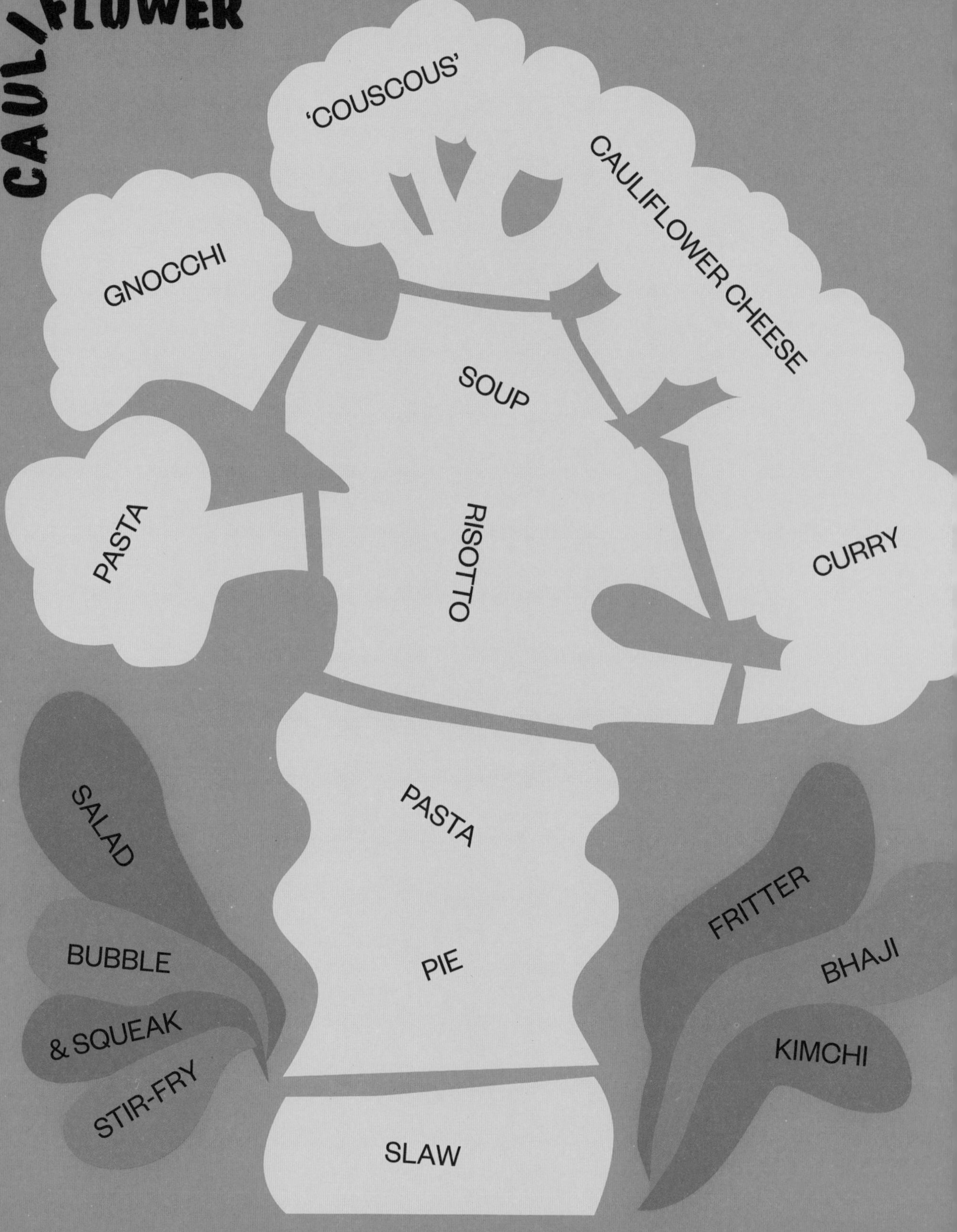

'COUSCOUS'

CAULIFLOWER CHEESE

GNOCCHI

SOUP

PASTA

RISOTTO

CURRY

SALAD

PASTA

BUBBLE

PIE

FRITTER

& SQUEAK

BHAJI

STIR-FRY

KIMCHI

SLAW

VEGETABLE SURGERY

Organic tastes better – it really does. Is your salad big enough to try yet (page 12)? Do you even want to try the pesticide-spray salad? I reckon you don't. Because organic tastes better and is better quality, the theory is that it is cheaper overall and uses less cooking time. Wait, that's not true... or is it?

Look at the cauliflower opposite. Or should I say look at the cauliflower florets, the stem and the leaves. Three different parts in one beautiful beast. Three different meals that you can eat, share or freeze for a rainy day. Eating food sustainably makes buying organic affordable.

Curried Cauliflower Stem Soup

Cauliflower Leaf Bhajis

SERVES 2

OLIVE OIL, FOR FRYING, PLUS EXTRA TO SERVE

2 ONIONS, CHOPPED

1 LEEK, SLICED

4 GARLIC CLOVES, SLICED

1 TBSP MEDIUM CURRY POWDER

CAULIFLOWER STEM, ROUGHLY CHOPPED

FEW GLUGS OF DOUBLE (HEAVY) CREAM

SALT

HANDFUL OF FRESH CORIANDER (CILANTRO), TO SERVE

Put some glugs of olive oil in a saucepan over a low–medium heat. Add the onions, leek, garlic and curry powder and sauté until soft.

Add the chopped cauliflower stem and season with salt. Cover the ingredients in the pan with cold water and boil for about 5–10 minutes until the cauliflower is soft. Pour some cream into the mix and whizz up in a food processor until smooth. Warm through the soup again and scatter with coriander and drizzle with extra olive oil to serve.

SERVES 2

CAULIFLOWER LEAVES, THINLY SLICED

2 ONIONS, THINLY SLICED

4 TBSP BROAD BEAN (FAVA BEAN) FLOUR OR CHICKPEA (GRAM) FLOUR

1 TBSP MADRAS CURRY POWDER

SALT

OIL WITH A HIGH SMOKING POINT SUCH AS RAPESEED OR SUNFLOWER, FOR DEEP-FRYING

Put the sliced cauliflower leaves and onions into a mixing bowl. Add the bean flour, madras curry powder and 6 tbsp of water. Season with salt and mix, adding more flour or water if necessary, until the mixture holds together well.

Add a good 2.5-cm/1-inch layer of oil to a heavy-bottomed saucepan over a medium heat. Heat the oil to 180°C/350°F, or until a piece of the batter sizzles and turns golden when dropped in. For each bhaji, pick up a tablespoonful of the mixture and carefully deposit it into the hot oil. Deep-fry the bhajis for about 2–3 minutes, turning a few times, until golden brown all over. Remove with a slotted spoon, drain the excess oil and serve.

Gnocchi with Cauliflower, Walnuts and Blue Cheese

SERVES 4

FOR THE GNOCCHI

500 G/1 LB 2 OZ LARGE POTATOES (FLOURY VARIETIES WORK WELL, OR USE WHATEVER IS IN SEASON)

170 G/6 OZ/1¼ CUPS PLAIN (ALL-PURPOSE) FLOUR (I ALSO SOMETIMES USE SPELT FLOUR), PLUS EXTRA FOR DUSTING THE WORK SURFACE

1 EGG

5 GRATES OF WHOLE NUTMEG

FOR THE SAUCE

LARGE KNOB OF SALTED BUTTER

FLORETS FROM 1 CAULIFLOWER, ROUGHLY CHOPPED

GENEROUS DASH OF WHITE WINE (OR SOME FINELY GRATED LEMON ZEST)

100 G/3½ OZ BLUE CHEESE

100 ML/3⅓ FL OZ/⅓ CUP DOUBLE (HEAVY) CREAM

LARGE BUNCH OF FRESH PARSLEY, ROUGHLY CHOPPED

SALT

TO SERVE

GOOD-QUALITY OLIVE OIL

LARGE HANDFUL OF LOCALLY GROWN NUTS (WALNUTS ARE BRILLIANT IN THIS RECIPE)

Preheat the oven to 200°C fan/220°C/425°F/gas mark 7.

Roast your large potatoes in the oven for 1 hour and then leave to cool for 15 minutes. Cut the potatoes in half, scoop out the flesh and add to a mixing bowl (save the skins for roasting with paprika and making into moreish crisps). Add the flour, egg, nutmeg and a pinch of salt. Use your hands to combine the mixture into a dough, then turn out onto a lightly floured work surface and knead through until silky smooth.

Cut the gnocchi dough into four pieces. On a lightly floured work surface, roll each piece into a long sausage, using both palms of your hands, until they're about 1 cm/½ inch in diameter. Cut the dough sausages into 2.5-cm/1-inch pieces and set aside.

Put a large saucepan of salted water on to boil ready for the gnocchi.

Meanwhile, put the butter in a large frying pan (skillet) over a medium heat. Add the roughly chopped cauliflower florets and sauté until soft. Add the white wine (or lemon zest) and cook for 1 minute. Add the blue cheese, cream and roughly chopped parsley and stir until melted together. Leave to one side.

Drop all the gnocchi into the boiling pan of water. Let them simmer for 3–5 minutes, and once they've floated to the surface and been there for a minute they are ready. Remove using a slotted spoon and add to the cauliflower cream sauce with a little of the cooking water from the pan. Turn the heat back up under the sauce, stir and leave for 2 minutes for the flavours to meld.

Portion into serving bowls, scatter over the nuts and finish with a final drizzle of good-quality olive oil.

TIP

If there are too many gnocchi, you can freeze them once boiled: just drizzle each one with a little oil and put in a container in the freezer. Defrost before using.

10

FORAGE, HUNT AND GATHER

Free food! Well, actually, it's just not sold in supermarkets.

Foraging is fantastic – the desire to go out and hunt for something has a sense of adventure and is a pleasant activity in itself. Think long spring walks, a splash of hope in the air and a pair of gloves in your hands in search of nettles and wild garlic. Lazy autumnal days with tawny, brown trees overhead, brambles covered in blackberries and elder dotted with berries. Sunny summer afternoons lingering down long winding paths perfumed with elderflower, snacking on sweet and sour wild strawberries as you go.

It's about finding the gems in the rough, and gems they are. They taste delicious and almost foreign because they're wild and not part of our everyday flavour repertoire. They're also incredibly nutritious – I actually warded off a nasty cold just by drinking elderberry juice every day. I have to admit it had fermented slightly so there was a taint of vinegar and alcohol which was a bit odd first thing in the morning, but it worked.

With all foraging, be respectful of your community, neighbours and the environment, and make sure you know what it is you're picking.

Best-ever Crumble Topping

This recipe has funny memories for me. I left it handwritten for my chefs to make one morning. I arrived at lunch and found them all making a seriously large conveyor belt of crumble topping, kilos and kilos of the stuff. They hadn't seen the middle commas in the amount of flour and butter, making over 40 kilos of crumble topping! This recipe does make more than you need for one serving, but you can store it in airtight containers for up to 3 months, lasting you the crumble season.

MAKES ENOUGH FOR ABOUT 10 CRUMBLES

400 G/14 OZ/3 CUPS PUMPKIN SEEDS

400 G/14 OZ/3 CUPS SUNFLOWER SEEDS

400 G/14 OZ CHOPPED LOCALLY SOURCED NUTS

400 G/14 OZ/4¼ CUPS ROLLED OATS

1.6 KG/3½ LB/12¾ CUPS PLAIN (ALL-PURPOSE) FLOUR

1 KG/2¼ LB/9 STICKS UNSALTED BUTTER, CUBED

1.3 KG/3 LB/6½ CUPS CASTER (SUPERFINE) SUGAR

20 G/¾ OZ GROUND CINNAMON

Preheat the oven to 160°C fan/180°C/350°F/gas mark 4.

Spread the pumpkin and sunflower seeds and chopped nuts out on a baking sheet. Bake in the oven 5–10 minutes. Leave to one side to cool but leave the oven on.

Mix the oats, flour, butter, sugar and cinnamon together in a mixing bowl and rub together using your fingertips to form rough breadcrumbs. Spread out over another baking sheet and roast for 15 minutes. Remove from the oven and stir, then roast for another 10 minutes. Leave to cool.

Mix the oat mixture thoroughly with the nut and seed mixture; this is your crumble topping. Once this is made you can store it in airtight containers for up to 3 months. It'll then only need 10 minutes in the oven on top of your stewed fruit.

Elderflower Cordial

Elderberry Syrup

The beauty of cordials is that they really capture the produce of the season, and that moment when everything is abundant and the garden is full of life. Elderflowers have a delicious, unique flavour that pairs so well with summer berries, especially strawberries.

It's wonderful how nature works. When different types of produce grow at the same time in the same season their flavours seem to work well together too. Elderberries have a taste somewhere between a blackberry and a blackcurrant, and they are a fantastic autumnal crop that goes well with other rich flavours like chestnuts, dark green brassicas, golden squash and game-like venison and pigeon. This syrup is also great as a cordial or for drizzling over fruit in a crumble.

MAKES 1.5 LITRES/2⅓ PINTS/GENEROUS 6 CUPS

1 KG/2 LB 4 OZ/5 CUPS CASTER (SUPERFINE) SUGAR

2 LEMONS

15 FRESH ELDERFLOWER HEADS

EQUIPMENT
MUSLIN (CHEESECLOTH)
STERILIZED GLASS BOTTLES

MAKES APPROX. 2 LITRES/3½ PINTS/8½ CUPS

1 KG/2 LB 4 OZ ELDERBERRIES

CASTER (SUPERFINE) SUGAR

EQUIPMENT
STERILIZED GLASS BOTTLES

In a large saucepan, dissolve the sugar in 650 ml/ 22 fl oz/2¾ cups water and bring to a simmer. Once simmering, grate in the zest from the lemons, then cut the lemons in half, squeeze their juices into the pan and add the lemon halves as well. Clean the elderflower heads and remove any rough stalks, then add these to the pan. Turn off the heat.

Leave the contents of the pan overnight to infuse. The next morning, strain the cordial through a muslin and store in sterilized bottles. The cordial will keep in the fridge for 3–6 months.

Place your berries into a saucepan. Pour over enough water to cover the berries, plus 2.5 cm/1 inch. Bring to a simmer (but do not let boil) for 20 minutes. Smash the berries a little with a metal spoon. Strain the liquid through a sieve (strainer) back into the saucepan and use the back of a spoon to squeeze more liquid out of the berries.

For every 100 ml/3⅓ fl oz/⅓ cup of liquid add 50 g/ 1¾ oz/4 tbsp sugar and stir to thoroughly dissolve while the liquid is still hot. Leave the syrup to cool and then store in sterilized bottles. It will keep for 3–6 months in a cool dark place or, even better, in the fridge.

Nettle and Spelt Risotto with Rainbow Chard and Cobnuts

I love the decadent taste of cobnuts, but filberts and hazelnuts are varieties of the same *Corylus* family, and almonds or walnuts also work in this delicious foraging dish, so you can use whatever is locally available. Nettles are incredibly prolific with huge amounts of nutrients. First brought to the UK by the Romans, they were used as a defense mechanism, and it's not hard to see why. But get yourself a sturdy pair of gloves and you can pluck away with ease.

SERVES 4

1 LARGE BAG OR 2 LARGE HANDFULS NETTLES

GOOD-QUALITY OLIVE OIL, FOR FRYING, PLUS EXTRA FOR DRIZZLING

2 ONIONS, DICED

6 GARLIC CLOVES, DICED

1 LEEK, DICED

HANDFUL OF PARSLEY, STALKS AND LEAVES SEPARATED AND CHOPPED

300 G/10½ OZ/GENEROUS 1¾ CUPS DRIED SPELT GRAINS

100 ML/3⅓ FL OZ/⅓ CUP WHITE WINE OR 4 TBSP VINEGAR OF YOUR CHOICE

200 G/7 OZ RAINBOW CHARD, ROUGHLY CHOPPED

SALT

TO SERVE

100 G/3½ OZ COBNUTS OR OTHER LOCALLY GROWN NUTS, ROUGHLY CHOPPED

HARD CHEESE, GRATED

Remove the nettle leaves from their stems using gloves and finely dice the green stems – removing any dirty or red stems first. Leave them both to one side separated.

Put a large saucepan over a medium heat and add a few glugs of oil. Add the diced onions, garlic, leek, parsley stalks and nettle stalks to the pan and sauté until soft. Add the spelt and season with salt. Add the wine or vinegar and cook for 1 further minute.

Cook the spelt like a risotto and slowly add 1.2 litres/generous 2 pints/5 cups of cold water, a ladle at a time, waiting until each addition is absorbed before adding the next. The whole process should take about 40 minutes.

When all the water is incorporated and the spelt is tender, add the chopped rainbow chard, parsley leaves and nettle leaves and stir for 1 minute over the heat or until the leaves have softened to your liking. Adjust the seasoning and add a little more water to loosen, if needed.

Portion the risotto into bowls and serve scattered with chopped nuts, a final drizzle of good olive oil and some grated hard cheese.

Barbecued Crayfish

Crayfish Bisque

Britain's rivers are full of the American variety of crayfish that were first introduced in the 70s, ironically as a programme to farm as a source of food. Nowadays, they're seen more as a pest killing our native crayfish - so we do our bit by cooking them at the pub in our wood-fired oven, drizzled with garlic oil and served with pink sauce.

Now to use the shells…

SERVES 4

100 G/3½ OZ/1 STICK MINUS 1 TBSP SALTED BUTTER

OIL OF YOUR CHOICE, FOR FRYING

2 SHALLOTS, DICED

1 LEEK, DICED

1 FENNEL BULB, DICED

500 G/1 LB 2 OZ PLUM OR CANNED TOMATOES

LEFTOVER CRAYFISH SHELLS FROM 1.2 KG/2¾ LB LIVE CRAYFISH (SEE LEFT)

1 FRESH BAY LEAF

100 ML/3⅓ FL OZ/⅓ CUP DOUBLE (HEAVY) CREAM

SALT

SERVES 2 AS A MAIN OR 4 AS AN APPETIZER

1.2 KG/2¾ LB LIVE CRAYFISH

6 GARLIC CLOVES, FINELY CHOPPED

GENEROUS PINCH OF SALT

200 ML/6¾ FL OZ/GENEROUS ¾ CUP OLIVE OIL

2 FRESH BAY LEAVES

MAYONNAISE AND TOMATO KETCHUP, TO SERVE (OPTIONAL)

EQUIPMENT

BARBECUE (GRILL)

Put the butter and a few good glugs of oil in a large saucepan and melt over a low–medium heat. Add the diced shallots, leek and fennel and sauté until soft.

Add the tomatoes and 200 ml/6¾ fl oz/generous ¾ cup of cold water and cook for 5 minutes, using a spoon to smash the tomatoes as they cook. Add the crayfish shells and bay leaf and cover with water plus 2.5 cm/ 1 inch. Bring to a simmer and cook for about 1 hour, topping up the water if needed.

Strain the liquid and put back into a large saucepan. Add the cream and reduce over a medium–high heat until the bisque is the consistency of single (light) cream. Season well with salt and serve.

Fire up your barbecue.

Fill your largest saucepan with water and bring to the boil. Drop in the live crayfish and boil for 3–5 minutes until bright red, then drain in a colander. Run cold water over them to cool them rapidly. Using a large, knife cut the crayfish in half lengthways and smash the claws with the back of a knife so they are easier to get into later.

Place the crayfish halves on a tray. Mix the garlic with the salt and oil, then drizzle over the crayfish. Throw a couple of bay leaves into the embers on the barbecue to release some flavour. Add the crayfish to the barbecue and cook for 5–10 minutes on each side until charred. Take them off using tongs and serve with cocktail sticks or a shellfish fork (saving the shells for the next recipe). Pink sauce is delicious with them, simply half mayo, half ketchup mixed.

11

PRESERVING FOR HUNGRY TIMES

Gluts are when plants grow like teenagers and lose control of their extending limbs, creating mountains of food that we can either eat in season or preserve for the future.

There are generally three seasons for a cook: 'the hungry gap', the time of plenty and the time to harvest and preserve. We'll find out on page 123 about the season called the hungry gap. It's basically a pretty annoying time when the new season's growth isn't ready to eat, and last year's

crops have either been eaten or are unusable. We know that this time exists, so to prepare for it we need to make 'hay whilst the sun shines' and preserve food.

The great thing about preserving is that you're creating flavour for the future – you can have peace of mind that something you have stored away will suddenly make a dish delicious, or add that last little zing you need, or is just the thing that will make a last-minute sandwich sing. You'll be envious of your future self!

Tomato Ketchup

MAKES ABOUT 2 KG/4½ LB

2 KG/4½ LB RED TOMATOES

OIL, FOR FRYING

4 RED ONIONS, ROUGHLY CHOPPED

1 CELERY HEAD OR FENNEL BULB, ROUGHLY CHOPPED

1 WHOLE GARLIC BULB, ROUGHLY CHOPPED

SMALL BUNCH OF BASIL, STALKS ROUGHLY CHOPPED (SAVE THE LEAVES FOR SOMETHING ELSE)

CHUNK OF FRESH GINGER, ROUGHLY CHOPPED

1 STAR ANISE

4 CLOVES

1 CINNAMON STICK

200 ML/6¾ FL OZ/GENEROUS ¾ CUP RED WINE VINEGAR OR APPLE JUICE

150 G/5½ OZ/¾ CUP LIGHT BROWN SOFT SUGAR

SALT AND FRESHLY GROUND BLACK PEPPER

EQUIPMENT
STERILIZED GLASS BOTTLES OR JARS

Preheat the oven to 200°C fan/220°C/425°F/gas mark 7.

Spread half the tomatoes out on a baking pan and roast for 30 minutes in the oven. Leave to cool.

Put some oil in a large saucepan over a low–medium heat. Add the chopped red onions, celery or fennel, garlic, basil stalks and ginger and sauté until soft and beginning to caramelize (but not colour too much). Roughly chop the remaining raw tomatoes and add these to the pan along with the roasted tomatoes, star anise, cloves, cinnamon stick, vinegar or apple juice and brown sugar. Pour in 300 ml/10 fl oz/1¼ cups of cold water and simmer over a low heat for about 45 minutes until reduced by half.

Remove the cloves and star anise, then blend in a food processor until smooth. Season and reduce more if you like it thicker. Decant into sterilized glass bottles or jars and leave to cool. Store in the fridge for up to 3 months.

Mushroom Ketchup

This has a nice savoury flavour, and I sometimes use it instead of soy sauce.

MAKES ABOUT 150 ML/5 FL OZ/⅔ CUP

1 KG/2 LB 4 OZ PORTOBELLO MUSHROOMS, SLICED

SALT

1 TSP GROUND GINGER

1 TSP GROUND ALLSPICE

3 CLOVES

1 TSP GROUND NUTMEG

20 PEPPERCORNS

10 JUNIPER BERRIES

20 G/¾ OZ/1 TBSP CASTER (SUPERFINE) SUGAR

EQUIPMENT
STERILIZED BOTTLES OR JARS

Find a container that will hold all the mushrooms, but at the same time something not too large. Layer the mushrooms in the container, sprinkling a good helping of salt between each layer. Once full, cover with a clean kitchen cloth and leave at room temperature for 24 hours.

Squeeze all the juice out of the mushrooms and put the flesh to one side – these are good for compost. You should have a nice amount of mushroom liquid – simmer this with all the spices and sugar for 10 minutes.

Leave to cool and infuse in the pan for a final 10 minutes before straining and bottling. Store at room temperature for up to 6 months.

Pickled Cucumbers

Beetroot Jam

I have some Danish blood in my family, so we have always celebrated Scandinavian flavours and traditions, which is why I love this recipe. These pickled cucumbers are amazing and perfect with any fish, especially in a fish finger sandwich - they also go wonderfully in a tartare sauce.

MAKES 1 LARGE JAR

200 G/7 OZ/1 CUP CASTER (SUPERFINE) SUGAR

450 ML/15 FL OZ/SCANT 2 CUPS WHITE WINE VINEGAR

1 TBSP PINK PEPPERCORNS

PINCH OF SALT

4 CUCUMBERS, SLICED INTO ROUNDS

1 BUNCH OF FRESH DILL

EQUIPMENT

LARGE STERILIZED MASON/KILNER JAR

Put the sugar, vinegar, peppercorns and a pinch of salt in a saucepan and bring to the boil to dissolve the sugar. Remove from the heat and leave to cool completely.

Layer the slices of cucumber with the dill in a mason/Kilner jar, and then pour over the cooled vinegar to cover. Store in the fridge and keep for 3–6 months.

The sweet, sharp, earthy flavour of this jam is great with a cheese board or in sandwiches.

MAKES ABOUT 1 KG/2 LB 4 OZ

500 G/1 LB 2 OZ RAW BEETROOT, TOPS REMOVED FOR ANOTHER DISH

500 G/1 LB 2 OZ RED ONIONS

250 ML/8½ FL OZ/GENEROUS 1 CUP CIDER VINEGAR OR RED WINE VINEGAR

250 ML/8½ FL OZ/GENEROUS 1 CUP SHARP APPLE JUICE OR RED WINE

500 G/1 LB 2 OZ/2½ CUPS CASTER (SUPERFINE) SUGAR

EQUIPMENT

STERILIZED JARS

Grate all the beetroot and thinly slice all the red onions – or use a food processor to finely chop them.

Mix together the vinegar, juice or red wine, sugar, beetroot and onions in a large saucepan. Simmer over a low heat for 2 hours. Every now and again, use a wooden spoon to move the mixture around, cooking until most of the liquid has disappeared and a delicious, sticky chutney is left. Decant into sterilized jars. Store in the fridge and keep for 3–6 months.

Flavoured Vinegars

Flavoured Oils

By trying to use or preserve everything in the pub kitchen, we always have an inspiring array of flavours to hand. These are great to have in moments of need when it's raining in January and you're craving a little bit of freshness. The tarragon vinegar, for example, is ideal for making a béarnaise sauce, and the dill is perfect in a sauce for fish.

Flavoured oils are also a fantastic store cupboard addition that can transform pastas or salad dressings or even make a deliciously novel off-the-cuff mayonnaise. There are two ways to make flavoured oils - the first is a cold infusion, made by simply cutting, crunching or bashing the produce to release the aromas, combining with oil and leaving for a few months. For this you can use produce like basil stalks or citrus peelings. If you have a food processor you can speed up the process by whizzing up your oil and produce, leaving for a few days, then straining and using. The second way is a hot infusion. This is best for flavours that need gently seducing out of their bodies, and/or need a cooking process to remove the chance of mould. For a warm infusion, don't heat the oil up too high otherwise it will become rancid, under 50°C/122°F is best. Homemade chilli oil is a must:

MILD VINEGAR OF YOUR CHOICE

FRESH HERBS OF YOUR CHOICE, SUCH AS TARRAGON, FENNEL, DILL OR ELDERFLOWER

EQUIPMENT

STERILIZED MASON/KILNER JARS

Fill your jars almost to the top with vinegar and add lots of whatever herbs you like. We make tarragon, fennel, elderflower and dill at the pub.

500 ML/17 FL OZ/2 CUPS LOCAL MILD-FLAVOURED OIL

5 LONG RED CHILLIES, SLICED

30 G/1 OZ DRIED CHILLI FLAKES (HOT RED PEPPER FLAKES)

EQUIPMENT

STERILIZED MASON/KILNER JARS

Put all the ingredients into a pan and slowly bring up the heat. Take off the heat and leave to infuse for at least 30 minutes. Once cool, strain and bottle.

12 STORING FOR A RAINY DAY

Summer is the time to grow, autumn is the time to harvest and during winter we store food until we need it. Dried broad beans (fava beans), cannellini beans, lentils, split peas and all other legumes and pulses can be stored away for months and months. Keeping them in mason/Kilner jars is both beautiful and practical, but any sealed container you can reuse, like jam jars, works just as well.

Our English summer provides massive gluts of beans that are then dried on the plants in the, hopefully, summer sun, which locks all the really important nutrients into the beans, ready for us to use when we need them. These beautiful beans and pulses are FLAVOUR SPONGES. They soak up any flavour that they can, plus adding their own nutty taste, with a starchy shine, which makes them the perfect ingredient for a low-cost meal with maximum taste. Plus, they have fantastic amounts of fibre which we all need lots more of in our lives. I use beans grown locally to me, like broad (fava) and borlotti, but you can use most legumes in similar ways:

- Chickpeas
- Fava beans (broad beans)
- Lentils
- Split peas
- Butterbeans
- Cannellini beans
- Borlotti beans
- Marrowfat peas
- Badger peas
- Kidney beans
- Flageolet beans
- Pinto beans

What to freeze and how

Fruits Cut into slices (unless they are berries), squeeze lemon juice over and freeze. Use in smoothies, crumbles or stews

Peppers, aubergines (eggplant), squash, courgettes (zucchini) Cut up into slices, roast in glugs of oil until soft and then freeze

Potatoes Mashed or blanched potatoes freeze well. Don't freeze raw potatoes, instead store in a dark place to get the most from them

Root vegetables Carrots, beetroots and parsnips all freeze well

Tomatoes Freeze really well, whole or chopped

Herbs Chop them up, place them in ice cube trays, fill with oil and freeze until needed

TIP!

If you want to stop things from clumping together in the freezer then spread out and freeze on a tray first. Once frozen, it's safe to pack them into a lidded container and they won't stick together.

Local Hummus with Beetroot

No longer just the domain of chickpeas, hummus is a great dish that allows lots of versatility with different pulses, legumes or even vegetables. I also make a hummus with split peas on page 131. This particular recipe can also be used as topping for a pie - simply spread the hummus over your pie filling (like you would do with mashed potato on a shepherd's pie), then cook in the oven in the way you normally would. It would work well on the Chicken Leg, Blue Cheese and Nettle Pie (page 49).

SERVES 6

250 G/9 OZ/1½ CUPS DRIED BROAD BEANS (FAVA BEANS)

2-3 RAW RED BEETROOTS, TOPS REMOVED AND SAVED FOR ANOTHER DISH

4 GARLIC CLOVES

JUICE OF ½ LEMON OR 3 TBSP LOCALLY PRODUCED VINEGAR

2 TBSP TAHINI

100 ML/3⅓ FL OZ/⅓ CUP GOOD-QUALITY OLIVE OIL OR A LOCAL OIL

SALT

Soak the beans for 24 hours in lots of water before using.

Preheat the oven to 180°C fan/200°C/400°F/gas mark 6.

Put the beetroots in a roasting pan and roast in the oven for about 45 minutes. Let them cool and then peel. Set aside.

Drain the soaked beans and put in a large saucepan. Cover with lots more water and simmer for about 30 minutes or until soft. Drain again, but keep the cooking water.

Transfer the cooked beans to a food processor and add the roasted beetroots, garlic cloves, lemon juice or vinegar, tahini, olive oil and some salt to taste. Blitz until smooth, adding some of the bean cooking water until you achieve the right consistency. (Any leftover cooking water can be used in soups or stews as a stock.)

Paprika Bean Stew with Red Peppers

This a great meal to have when red peppers are in season, or perhaps you can use your own Homemade Paprika (page 85), preserved red peppers and jarred tomatoes for when summer veg supplies are meagre.

SERVES 2

FOR COOKING THE BEANS

200 G/7 OZ/SCANT 1¼ CUPS DRIED BEANS OF YOUR CHOICE (CANNELLINI OR BORLOTTI ARE GREAT HERE)

1 ONION, PEELED AND HALVED

3 FRESH BAY LEAVES

FOR THE STEW

OIL, FOR FRYING

2 ONIONS, DICED

6 GARLIC CLOVES, DICED

2 RED PEPPERS DESEEDED, STALKS REMOVED AND ROUGHLY CHOPPED (OR YOU CAN USE PRESERVED JARRED WHOLE PEPPERS, ROUGHLY CHOPPED)

1 TBSP HOMEMADE PAPRIKA (PAGE 85)

1 TBSP DRIED OREGANO

250 G/9 OZ TOMATOES, CANNED OR FRESH AND CHOPPED

SALT

LARGE BUNCH OF FRESH PARSLEY AND CHUNKS OF BREAD, TO SERVE

Soak the beans for 24 hours in lots of cold water before using.

Drain the beans and transfer to a large saucepan with 2 litres/3½ pints/generous 8½ cups of water, the onion and bay leaves. Cook over a medium heat for about 45–60 minutes until the beans are soft, topping up the water as needed. Drain again, reserving the cooking water but discarding the onion and bay leaves.

Put some glugs of oil in a large saucepan over a medium heat. Add the diced onions and garlic and sauté until soft.

Add the roughly chopped red peppers and season with salt – if you're using fresh peppers, continue cooking until they are soft and caramelized, but if you're using preserved peppers you can skip straight to the next stage. We want the peppers to be soft and squidgy – which brings out the sweetness and intensifies the flavour.

Add the paprika and oregano and cook for a further minute, then add the tomatoes. Add a ladle of the reserved bean cooking water, turn the heat to low–medium and simmer gently for 25 minutes. We're concentrating the flavours here, allowing them to meet and become great friends.

Add the beans to the tomato sauce and stir. Add another ladle of the reserved bean cooking water and continue cooking for another 15 minutes, allowing the beans to absorb the other flavours and release their own starch and creaminess.

Serve the stew, scatter with fresh parsley and eat with a chunk of bread to mop up the juices.

TIP

If you eat meat, this a great opportunity to be sustainable and use those parts of the animal that might normally be thrown away, like pork bones or leftover chicken from the wings. And if you're feeling particularly luxurious, small amounts of items like chorizo or cured ham can go a long way – only a little bit of chorizo will add delicious flavour and you can save the rest for tomorrow night's pizza topping.

POLLINATORS CAN DECIDE OUR FUTURE

Organic may feel like it costs more on your weekly shop, but non-organic will cost far, far more in years to come. Pesticides kill insects and if we didn't have insects, the pollination industry could be valued at £200 billion a year in the UK alone. That's an extra £3000 to our yearly spend per person. If pollinators disappear, food will become far more expensive than your organic avocado from the supermarket.

THREE THINGS YOU CAN DO IMMEDIATELY TO SAVE POLLINATORS

1. Buy organic – pesticides kill pests and also affect our buzzing bees. As discussed on page 53, cooking sustainably means that you can afford to buy organic.

2. Buy raw, local honey – from non-sugar-fed bees.

3. Grow flowers! And lots of them – in the garden, on your windowsills, on your roof, in the porch – everywhere!

Not all honey is equal

I believe in equality for everyone, including bees. So why have I written this?

It's pretty clear we need to cut down on the amount of sugar in our diets – by quite a lot actually. Honey is a more nutrient-dense form of sugar, which is why some people think that replacing sugar with honey solves all their problems. But just because it's a 'healthy sugar' doesn't mean that we can eat more than our recommended daily intake. Actually, that's the same with all sugar alternatives – it's still sugar, just in a different form.

Also, we can't ALL replace sugar with honey. If we did, our poor bees would be very tired. In addition to this, bee farmers feed bees with sugar over winter because they take all the honey, which in turn is making the bees ill in the same way too much sugar makes us ill. So when someone tells you to eat honey instead of sugar because it's healthier, try to choose local, raw honey from non-sugar-fed bees, which is more nutrient dense, super delicious and promotes the well-being of the bees.

TIP!
They also say if you eat a teaspoon of local honey it will help with any pollen-related allergies.

Bees vs diets

What is monoculture and why is it so bad? Monoculture is intensively growing a single crop or farming a single product in a given area. Monoculture is not sustainable – in fact it is detrimental to the earth's productivity and soil diversity. It normally occurs as a reaction to an incessant demand for a product that consumerism and materialism have created – more on this in a moment.

As we know, too much sugar is bad for one's health. It doesn't contain lots of necessary nutrients and overconsumption can lead to health problems like obesity, diabetes and tooth decay. In fact, sugar is to blame for a lot of the major health problems we have in society. What this does NOT mean is that a) sugar is evil and b) we should change our diets to replace all sugar with substitutes. What it actually means is that we should eat less sugar in all its forms – glucose, sucrose, fructose – and we should be told clearly where these sugars are.

Drinks like fruit juices contain high amounts of fructose in a concentrated level, which have a proven negative effect if taken in large quantities every day. The actual recommendation is 150 ml/5 fl oz per day of fruit or vegetable juice, which is hardly anything. The reason this is recommended is because fruit juice contains no fibre to help digest the fructose which normally exists in the fruit's pulp. So, by drinking a 250 ml/8½ fl oz plastic bottle of juice, not only are we causing damage to our bodies, but we're probably adding to the single-use plastic waste damaging our oceans and marine life.

Pollinators Can Decide Our Future

Screw the juice – just eat an amazing organic orange instead. From this we can consume the recommend daily allowance and also use the pulp and fibre to aid digestion. We can then use the orange skins to make snacks or orangecello (orange version of limoncello, page 36). And we haven't had to use single-use plastic! One simple change like this is a really positive and holistic step towards a sustainable future.

So we are all agreed that overconsumption of sugar is bad for us. What we really don't want to do though, as advertised by celebrity diet promoters, is to replace all sugar with honey. This is factually incorrect advice and also sustainably incorrect. Honey is sugar – it just has more nutrients. The main problem is that we are encouraged to see honey as just another limitless product to buy and consume, rather than as the fragile part of nature that it is.

Honey is the incredible creation of a very intelligent and hierarchal species that we still don't fully understand. It is full of nutrients, tastes amazing and the taste often reflects the source of the nectar. Bees are efficient, but hives are delicate and can't produce limitless amounts without human interference which is detrimental to them and to the quality of the honey itself. If we are to replace our use of sugar with honey, then that creates a monoculture, which negatively affects the species and its possible survival.

To keep up with the current demand for honey, producers have started to feed the bees sugar. Although this has successfully met our need for honey, the detrimental effect, along with the spraying of pesticides, has caused Colony Collapse Disorder, driving our beloved bees to near extinction. There is also more than a little irony in the fact that, knowing the damage that sugar does to our bodies, we have used it to feed the bodies making our sugar alternative.

So, within this very specific subject, we meet a point where sustainability and diets clash. Fad diets do not equal global health. And they certainly do not equal global sustainability. So perhaps instead of 'substituting', we should try to create better techniques for extracting the natural sweetness from ingredients. Many vegetables, for example, are rich in sugars – think of roasted red peppers, rich tomato sauce or the obvious sweet potatoes. Starch and carbohydrates contain sugar. So, the answer to this lies in changing our ways of cooking and rebalancing our palates. Sugar, like salt, is a seasoning. Perhaps we need to learn how to season again and think about how we can create sweetness from natural produce. I love honey – I really do, but it's not a life-given right to have honey all the time. Honey is to be respected and so are its makers.

'WE'RE SUBSTITUTING SUGAR WITH ANOTHER SUGAR PRODUCT AND DRIVING OUR BELOVED BEES TO NEAR EXTINCTION.'

Pollinators Can Decide Our Future

Warm Apple Terrine

This recipe is a beautiful expression of autumn flavours. It doesn't need any sugar, instead we're letting the ripe fruits speak for themselves. Eating fruit at the right time when it's naturally at its best means we can let the cooking process bring out the natural sweetness.

SERVES 8

15 VERY RIPE SWEET EATING APPLES, ROYAL GALA ARE DELICIOUS

150 G/5⅓ OZ/1¼ STICKS UNSALTED BUTTER, MELTED

CREAM AND RIPE BLACKBERRIES, TO SERVE

EQUIPMENT

20-CM/8-INCH LOAF PAN, WELL GREASED

Preheat the oven to 180°C fan/200°C/400°F/gas mark 6.

Peel, core and thinly slice the apples. Mix together in a bowl with the melted butter and layer them into the prepared loaf pan. Press down slightly to ensure they're compact, then wrap the pan in some foil. Bake for 1 hour 15 minutes. Remove from the oven and leave to cool for 20 minutes before turning out .

Slice and serve the terrine for dessert with cream and ripe blackberries.

My 30-mile Cake: Pear Cake with Caramelized Whey

Taste buds get accustomed to the daily routine of what we eat - if we were to cut out salt from our diets then most shop-bought food would taste too salty. Likewise with sugar, go back years and most desserts probably didn't taste very sweet, but they were fantastic to the people of the time. We have grown to love and adore sugar, it's such a delicious seasoning if used well, it gives us pleasure and it makes us feel rewarded. However, we do all need to reduce our intake drastically for all sorts of health reasons. Apple juice contains roughly 15 g/¾ oz of sugar per 100 ml/3⅓ fl oz, which is quite a lot, so we're going to use that as our sugar source in this cake. Whey and milk also have sugar content, so by caramelizing these we can also achieve a sweeter taste. This is a cake dedicated to using sugars from natural sources within 30 miles of us.

SERVES 8

FOR THE CARAMELIZED WHEY

2 LITRES/3½ PINTS/8½ CUPS WHOLE MILK

2 TSP VEGGIE RENNET

500 ML/17 FL OZ/2 CUPS DOUBLE (HEAVY) CREAM

¼ TBSP BICARBONATE OF SODA

FOR THE CAKE

1 KG/2 LB 4 OZ PEARS (OR EXPERIMENT WITH OTHER FRUITS), PLUS EXTRA TO SERVE

500 ML/17 FL OZ/2 CUPS SWEET APPLE JUICE

250 G/9 OZ/1¾ CUPS PLUS 2 TBSP PLAIN (ALL-PURPOSE) FLOUR

2 TSP BAKING POWDER

1 TSP BICARBONATE OF SODA

200 G/7 OZ/1¾ STICKS UNSALTED BUTTER, SOFTENED

4 EGGS

½ TSP MALDON SALT OR ¼ TSP REGULAR

EQUIPMENT

COOKING THERMOMETER

20-CM/8-INCH CAKE PAN, LIGHTLY OILED

Whey is a by-product of cheese making. To make it, put the milk in a large saucepan and heat to 38°C/100°F, measuring with a thermometer. Turn off the heat, stir in the rennet and leave for 30 minutes.

After this time, the curds and whey should have started to separate, with the curds floating to the top. Make six slices, three one way and three the other, in the curds that are resting on the top and leave for 15 minutes more. Using a slotted spoon, carefully remove the curds and leave to drain in a sieve (strainer), before storing them in the fridge for use in another recipe, like a cheesecake. The liquid left behind is the whey – you should get about 1.5 litres/2⅓ pints/generous 6 cups from this amount of milk.

Add the cream to the whey in the pan and bring to a simmer. Add the bicarbonate of soda, reduce the heat to very low and cook for about 1 hour, stirring occasionally. It will eventually turn chestnut brown with the consistency of thick cream. Remove from the heat and set aside.

Peel and core the pears and cut into cubes (keep the peelings to dehydrate for snacks). Add the pear cubes to a new saucepan with the apple juice and place over a high heat. Rapidly reduce until most of the juice disappears and the pears go a rich golden amber colour. Blitz the pears down in a food processor to make a purée.

Preheat the oven to 180°C fan/200°C/400°F/gas mark 6.

Put the flour, baking powder, bicarbonate of soda, softened butter, eggs and salt in a mixing bowl. Mix together with a hand-held electric whisk (or in a stand mixer with the beater attachment). Add 250 g/9 oz of the pear purée and mix to combine. Pour the batter into the oiled cake pan and bake for 30–40 minutes until a skewer inserted comes out clean.

Serve the cake drizzled with the caramelized whey, with the rest of the pear purée and some sliced fresh pears on the side.

LIFE IS NOT BLACK AND WHITE

And nor is food! Nature is all about reacting to what's in front of you and learning how to love it.

For years farmers have been throwing away wonky veg or ploughing it back into the ground because it hasn't met superficial supermarket standards. This is absurd! And makes the overall yield less for no good reason. Wonky veg should be glorified for all its quirkiness.

According to *The Lancet Report* (January 2019), vegetarianism is probably the most sustainable environmental eating option because it is associated with the greatest reduction in greenhouse gases, land and water use. Plant-based diets reduce emissions by 80%. So let's show our love for our planet by appreciating our wonky veg.

There is currently a great social movement concerning body positivity – encouraging everyone to be comfortable in their own unique and beautiful skins. Well, the same should apply for vegetables: Vegetable Body Positivity.

Use these hashtags to connect to other positive people and share your wonky veg ideas:

#veggiebodypositivity   #curvycucumber
#vegshapepositivity   #crookedcarrot
#nofilterveg   #askewapple
#nomatterwhatshape   #vegareequal

Of the 14,000 edible plant species only 150–200 are used by humans, only three of which (rice, maize and wheat) contribute to 60% of all food consumed by humans.

Best before vs use by dates

The difference between best before and use by is causing a lot of waste in our homes. Best before is about quality, not safety. The food will be safe to eat after this date but may not be at its best. It means you can turn it into stews or soups. The use by date on food is about safety. This is the most important date to remember as food after this time is dangerous and should be avoided. Correctly storing food below 5°C/40°F in your fridge will help guarantee the use by date is accurate.

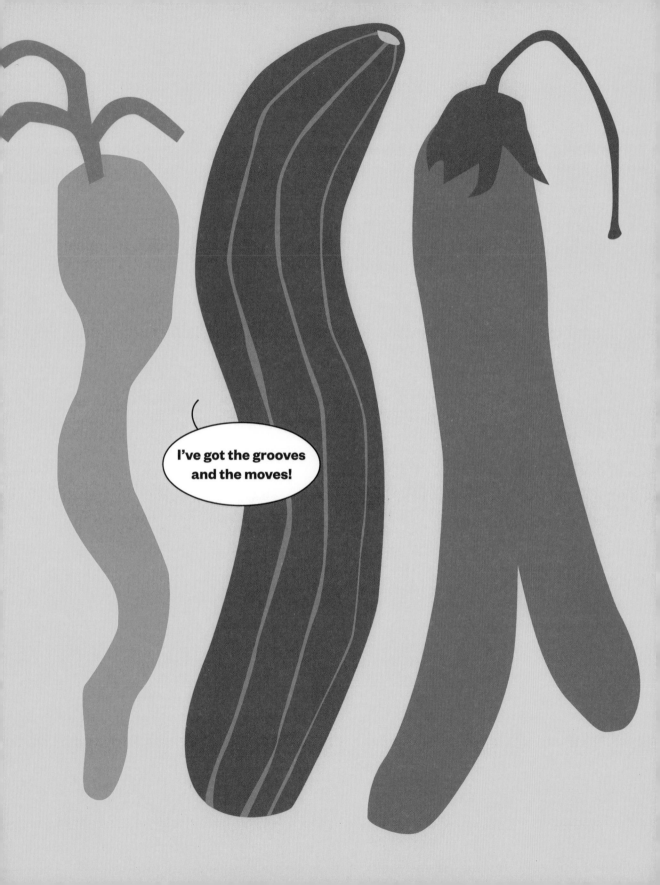

Wonky Chilli, Pepper and Tomato Shakshuka

There is something both comforting and adventurous about this Persian/North African dish. It warms the heart with its use of chilli, red pepper and paprika, and yet braising an egg in a stew adds a risk - whether you can cook all the white and keep the yolk soft. I find baking the eggs in the oven the most reliable method. Also, if you can use some slightly older eggs that will help… as eggs get older the white separates from the yolk which means the whites will cook faster! We also use this method when cooking eggs on pizzas. For perfect poached eggs, it's the opposite, you want the eggs to be as fresh as possible.

SERVES 4

OLIVE OIL, FOR FRYING

2 RED ONIONS, THINLY SLICED

2 GARLIC CLOVES, THINLY SLICED

1 WONKY CHILLI, SLICED

1 TSP PAPRIKA

1 TSP GROUND CUMIN

1 PINCH OF SAFFRON

2 WONKY RED PEPPERS, STALKS REMOVED AND DESEEDED, CUT INTO CHUNKS

8 WONKY TOMATOES, ROUGHLY CHOPPED (OR 1 X 400-G/14-OZ CAN OF TOMATOES)

4 SLIGHTLY OLDER EGGS

SALT

TO SERVE

BUNCH OF FRESH PARSLEY, ROUGHLY CHOPPED

GOOD-QUALITY BREAD

EQUIPMENT

LARGE, HEAVY-BOTTOMED OVENPROOF FRYING PAN (SKILLET)

Preheat the oven on to 180°C fan/200°C/400°F/gas mark 6.

Put some glugs of olive oil in the pan over a low–medium heat. Add the sliced red onions and garlic and sauté until soft. Add the sliced chilli to the pan with the spices and fry for 3–5 minutes, stirring. Add the chopped red peppers with a little more oil and cook for 20 minutes, stirring, slowly caramelizing them until they're sweet and soft.

Add the chopped tomatoes along with 100 ml/3⅓ fl oz/⅓ cup water. Cook for at least 15 minutes, allowing all the wonderful flavours to meet and greet. Season the sauce with salt and give it a stir. Now crack the eggs into the sauce and place the pan in the oven for 8–10 minutes or until the whites are cooked.

Carefully place the pan in the middle of the table on a heatproof surface. Sprinkle the shakshuka with chopped parsley and serve with some cracking bread to mop up the juices.

SPICE UP YOUR LIFE

I'm not going to lie, I love to travel. And I love to eat food from all over the world. Italian, Thai, Indian, Japanese, Moroccan, Brazilian, Spanish – it's all marvellous. I also get this craving to try new flavours and experiences; it's like a bug that every now and again I need to fix. So when I feel I shouldn't travel, I recreate the food at home.

There's nothing wrong with importing produce. In England we actually need it at certain times of the year (known as the hungry gap) because our soils don't produce much in this period. There are certain imported ingredients that add powerful flavour but don't have huge effects on the planet. The secret is to know what produce to eat from around you and what to buy.

FAIRTRADE

This organization sets the standard for equality and sustainability across the world. Eating food from around the world means being part of another culture and someone else's life – it helps us feel more connected to the world, and more importantly, to the people who've produced it. Let's celebrate these people by making sure they get the rewards they deserve! In their own words, this is what Fairtrade are all about:

- *Fairtrade supports local farms, local businesses and local people. It makes countries and the world stronger and more united.*
- *Workers on Fairtrade farms enjoy freedom of association, safe working conditions and sustainable wages. Forced child and slave labour are strictly prohibited.*
- *It guarantees that products are produced with limited amounts of pesticides and fertilizers, with proper management of waste, water and energy.*
- *Fairtrade believes in gender equality and its importance to social sustainability.*
- *It guarantees a fair price to farmers for their products, covering the cost of production and adding a premium which is invested in social or economic projects.*
- *Fairtrade sets social, economic and environmental standards for both companies and the farmers and workers who grow the food we love.*

Spices

My local curry house is one of the best. I think I ate there every month for about a year and I have no guilt. It's a real treat and a reward after a hard-working week. A good curry can set the world alight and ignite your taste buds. In the same way, a few spices can transform our local wonky vegetables into something fantastic. Spices add depth and flavour to all sustainable dishes and are great for health.

Dried spaghetti

One of my favourite meals is spaghetti vongole – it's one of the simplest dishes ever but it oozes with umami, salty, fresh flavours. All it is, is spaghetti, clams, garlic, white wine, parsley and olive oil. The secret to it is to buy the best quality spaghetti. With decent spaghetti you don't need a lot of other ingredients to make a really incredible meal, so overall it can work out as cheaper. When buying dried pasta – look for bronze die cut. This means that when the pasta is extruded, the machine creates a rough texture on the pasta to allow the most amount of sauce to stick to it. Better pasta equals happier lives.

Olive oil

I feel very lucky that I have two friends who produce their own organic olive oil, one from Tuscany and the other from Puglia. Each has a completely different flavour but they're equally delicious. They're so much more than just oil, they're like a seasoning and the perfect way to finish off many dishes. Don't scrimp on the price, buy the best. It'll transform your food and you can use cheaper oils for the majority of hot cooking.

Tomatoes

I love tomatoes. So versatile, and they are the beating heart of a lot of European cooking. We should only be importing canned tomatoes, and if you want the best, look for Strianese or San Marzano. Great for making food in the hungry gap more enticing.

Vinegars

You will find that there is always a local vinegar to you, whether it's apple, wine, malt, grape or grain-based. You can use these for a lot of cooking, but a really excellent artisan version is a thing of beauty. Matured and developed, it adds layers to your food and, like a good oil, it can make a dish.

Mustards

These add depth and heat to a dish. They have a distinctive flavour that we try to copy at the pub by using plants that have a similar taste like nasturtium flowers and mustard leaves. But sometimes these aren't available or a dish is just crying out for a kick of the real stuff.

Olives, capers and anchovies

There are certain ingredients that you just can't imitate. For me, olives, capers and anchovies are so expressive of the Mediterranean that it's hard to imagine the food without them. Capers are unique – you either love them or hate them – but once you fall in love, you'll fall hard. All of these add great saltiness and umami flavour.

Chocolate

I don't think there is anything quite like chocolate. In its raw state it is completely different to what we have grown to love and cherish, but once it has been processed into our store cupboard ingredient, it waits patiently for our very impatient cravings. Unfortunately, I'm not sure if there is much that can replicate chocolate, but buy organic and definitely Fairtrade. And never buy chocolate that uses palm oil – this causes massive deforestation and destruction of ecosystems. Chocolate is a luxury – let's start thinking about the welfare of the people who make it when we buy it.

Fruits

There is nothing better than a fresh, juicy sweet peach straight off the tree at the height of August – but there are also some amazing unique fruits all around the world that are delicious. Flavour combinations like passion fruit and chocolate, kiwi and goat's cheese, melon and seaweed or mulberries and bananas. Wouldn't life be boring without these... after all what are you going to put in your gin and tonic? Buy local fruits first, and imported fruits as a treat.

Coconuts

Sometimes, you just can't beat the sweet creaminess that coconut milk can add to curry or the lightness that coconut oil can add to a stir-fry. But it needs to be organic, non-GMO and responsibly harvested. The demand for coconuts means that mass-production is a real threat and potentially destroying rainforests.

A WORLD FOOD FIGHT

The demand for exported foods is at an all time high, but it does come at a price. Every time we grow from the land, it gives us nutrients. If we dig up and export these around the world, without giving anything back to the earth, we end up with decreased soil fertility. At times it feels as though we are ripping our countries apart and tossing them around the world to satisfy our appetites. As much as I love exported food, it should be viewed as much more of a luxury than is currently the case.

Homemade Worcestershire Sauce

MAKES ABOUT 1 LITRE/1¾ PINTS/4 CUPS

OIL, FOR FRYING

2 ONIONS, SLICED

6 GARLIC CLOVES, THINLY SLICED

250 ML/8½ FL OZ/GENEROUS 1 CUP APPLE CIDER VINEGAR

100 G/3½ OZ APPLE MOLASSES (SEE BELOW)

100 G/3½ OZ HONEY

500 ML/17 FL OZ/2 CUPS WATER

100 G/3½ OZ GOLDEN CASTER (SUPERFINE) SUGAR

200 ML/6¾ FL OZ/GENEROUS ¾ CUP BEER OR ALE

3 CLOVES

EQUIPMENT

STERILIZED BOTTLES OR JARS

Put a few glugs of oil in a large saucepan and cook the onions over a low–medium heat until soft and sweet.

Add the rest of the ingredients and simmer for about 45 minutes until thick enough to coat the back of a spoon. Blitz up in a food processor and then pass through a sieve (strainer). Decant into sterilized bottles or jars and store at room temperature for up to 3–6 months.

TIP: HOMEMADE MOLASSES

Instead of buying in imported molasses for use in recipes, why not get creative and make your own? Molasses is simply the result of the slow, patient reduction of a juice or alcohol, until it's as thick as honey. You will need to remember to stir occasionally so as not to scorch the bottom of the pan.

In places like Persia, pomegranates are used for pomegranate reduction; in Italy they make balsamic wine reduction. It's a shame that we get so hooked on international products when we have so much beautiful produce to use in our own countries, so use what fruits you have around you. England has so many apples and we export a ridiculous amount. My dad makes his own cider, so in my case I reduce that to make wonderful apple molasses. If you've never heard of or tried 'black butter' I urge you to look into it. It's a reduction of cider, apples and spices that has an amazing wintery flavour, full of rich sweet and sour notes and great as a marinade.

Caponata

Caponata is in my top 10 dishes of all time - it is the pure expression of a late summer harvest. Here I'm using imported capers and olives, because without them it just isn't the same. It is delicious by itself, with roast lamb or barbecued mackerel or even as a pasta sauce.

SERVES 4 OR 6 AS A PASTA SAUCE

150 ML/5 FL OZ/⅔ CUP OLIVE OIL

2 RED ONIONS, ROUGHLY CHOPPED

6 GARLIC CLOVES, ROUGHLY CHOPPED

LARGE BUNCH OF FRESH MARJORAM AND ITS FLOWERS, FINELY CHOPPED

LARGE BUNCH OF FRESH BASIL, LEAVES AND STALKS SEPARATED, FINELY CHOPPED

2 AUBERGINES (EGGPLANTS), DICED INTO 2.5-CM/1-INCH CUBES

500 G/1 LB 2 OZ RIPE TOMATOES, FINELY CHOPPED

2 TBSP CAPERS

3 TBSP PITTED BLACK OLIVES

SALT

Put the olive oil in a saucepan over a low–medium heat. Add the chopped red onions and garlic to the pan and cook slowly in all the oil until soft.

Add the finely chopped marjoram and basil stalks. Add the diced aubergines – they will absorb the flavoured oil as well as releasing their own juices. Season with salt and cook down slowly for about 30 minutes until the aubergine flesh is soft but still with a little structure.

Add the chopped tomatoes. Turn the heat to medium and simmer for about 15–20 minutes. If you need to add a little water to loosen the ingredients, then please do. Finally, add the capers, olives and basil leaves. Check and adjust the seasoning if needed and serve.

Homemade Paprika

MAKES ABOUT 20 G/¾ OZ

5 RED ROMANO PEPPERS

EQUIPMENT

DEHYDRATOR (OPTIONAL)

Very simply cut the peppers into slices, remove the pith, seeds and stalks. Dehydrate the pepper slices in a dehydrator or in your oven on the lowest temperature setting. It'll probably take about 10 hours, but keep going until the peppers are totally dry.

Blend the dried peppers to very fine crumbs in a spice grinder or food processor with a strong, high-speed motor. Store the paprika in an airtight container for up to 3 months.

TIP

Smoked paprika is even more delicious, it uses the same technique but first the peppers are lightly smoked on a wood fire or barbecue (grill).

Salted Chocolate Orange Tart

This recipe is absolutely delicious, and it uses two great imported products – chocolate and orange. But to make this tart even better, we're going to add an ingredient that has taken the pastry and ice cream worlds by storm in the last five years: salt. A little amount of salt in caramel or chocolate can elevate the way you taste sweetness to new levels. One of the best times I ever made this recipe was when I accidentally lost track of time and I was late in creating it for a dinner party. With only one hour until the guests arrived and knowing that the tart had to set before we could eat it, I was on the wrong side of tense. But what I hadn't anticipated was how luxurious this tart is if it has only just set and is still a little warm. Luckily, my guests ate their main courses slowly. This is just the filling, so find a sweet pastry recipe that works for you.

SERVES 6-8

200 G/7 OZ/1¾ STICKS UNSALTED BUTTER

200 G/7 OZ/1 CUP MUSCOVADO SUGAR

1 TSP SEA SALT

FINELY GRATED ZEST OF 1 ORANGE, PLUS PARED ORANGE ZEST, TO GARNISH (OPTIONAL)

200 ML/6¾ FL OZ/GENEROUS ¾ CUP DOUBLE (HEAVY) CREAM

200 G/7 OZ MILK CHOCOLATE

FOR THE PASTRY CASE

250 G/9 OZ/2 CUPS PLAIN (ALL-PURPOSE) FLOUR, PLUS EXTRA FOR DUSTING

125 G/4 OZ/1 STICK PLUS 1 TBSP UNSALTED BUTTER, COLD

75 G/3 OZ/½ CUP CASTER SUGAR

1 EGG

50 ML/1¾ FL OZ/3½ TBSP COLD WATER

EQUIPMENT

1 X 25-CM/10-INCH LOOSE-BOTTOMED TART TIN, GREASED WITH BUTTER OR OIL

First, make your pastry case. Sift the flour into a large mixing bowl and add the sugar. Cut the cold butter into cubes, add to the bowl and, using your fingertips, gently work it into the flour and sugar until the mixture resembles breadcrumbs (alternatively, pulse it all together in a food processor). Add the egg and water and gently work it together until it forms a ball of dough. Remember not to work the pastry too much at this stage or it will become tough. Sprinkle with a little flour, place on a plate and cover with a kitchen cloth. Leave in the fridge for 30 minutes.

Dust a clean work surface with flour and then carefully roll out your pastry, turning it every so often, until it's about ½ cm/¼ inch thick and will cover the tin and sides. Carefully lift the pastry onto the tin and centre it. Ease the pastry into the tin, making sure you push it into all the sides – a little bit of excess pastry rolled into a ball is good for doing this. Trim away the excess with a sharp knife, prick the base of the pastry and pop it back in the fridge while you get the oven to temperature.

Preheat the oven to 180°C fan/200°C/400°F/gas mark 6.

Pop some baking parchment, large enough to cover the tart, over the pastry, fill with baking beans and bake for 15 minutes. Then remove your beans and parchment from the pastry case and bake again for a further 5 minutes. Leave to cool.

Now, for the filling. In a saucepan, add the butter and muscovado sugar and place over a medium heat. Simmer for 2–3 minutes, before stirring in the salt, orange zest and cream. Bring to the boil, then simmer for 2 minutes. Remove from the heat and whisk in the chocolate until melted. Pour this mixture into the tart case and leave in the fridge for 2 hours to set (if it doesn't get the full 2 hours, it's still incredibly delicious while still a little warm). Bring the tart back to room temperature an hour before you want to serve. Garnish with extra pared orange zest if you like.

50% OF WITHIN

20 Snacks Relax

21 Make Your Favourite Meal Challenge

16 Super Not-So-Super Foods

17 Fat

22 We Need Flies to Have Lions

18 Gluten

19 Dairy

23 The Hungry Gap

50% from 30 miles

How can this work in cities, I hear you ask. How can millions of people eat food produced within 30 miles?

Let's turn the question around and imagine how lovely our cities would look if we did. Imagine cities filled with wild flowers for bees, where every garden has vegetables growing, every porch has herbs in pots. Let's not see this as a challenge but as the solution to making our lives more beautiful.

I believe that we're using spaces inefficiently, and by making some changes and using some new techniques, we can all live more sustainably.

SUPER NOT-SO-SUPER FOODS

Even their title undermines all other foods. If I'm not Superman or Batman, then I'm just a mere person walking the streets, waiting for my super hero to save me from destruction. These characters are fictional and I'm afraid so is the story associated with our new super-food friends.

When quinoa was grown in the Andes by Incas using their intelligent farming skills and knowledge, it probably was super good for them. It provided them with the slow-burning energy and nutrients that allowed their civilization to prosper and succeed. However nice this story is, it doesn't mean that mass farming of pesticide-sprayed quinoa grown anywhere is just as wonderful. On the contrary, if something is mass farmed then it is unlikely that the soil will be able to give it the same rich nutrients, year after year.

Food is amazing. All foods have the ability to save us if grown properly and taken in the right proportion. All food is super food as it gives us energy. Without food we would have no life and no pleasure.

Strawberry: 'I was doing really well until the goji berry came along. People liked me, even loved me. I was at the top of my game. Now all people want is some lady called aunty oxidants. I hear the lead singer is a blueberry.'

Pumpkin Seed: 'Me and my mates were the best band in the 90s... together we were The 3 Seeds. Sunflower on the bass, Lin on the drums and me on guitar and vocals. Now there's this guy called Chia who's stolen the limelight. I reckon he's just a fad. I hope so anyway, otherwise we're out of the game!'

Here are some very local foods to eat that have the same properties as imported 'super foods':

For omega-3s Instead of chia seeds, eat sunflower seeds, pumpkin seeds, linseeds

For fats with vitamins and high smoking point Instead of coconut oil, use rapeseed oil, grapeseed oil or sunflower oil. (The British Nutrition Foundation has said that there is no strong scientific evidence to support health benefits from eating coconut oil)

For slow-releasing energy Instead of quinoa, eat pearl barley, whole spelt or jumbo oats

For vitamin C Instead of goji or acai berries, eat strawberries or raspberries

For protein Instead of imported almonds, use local nuts such as walnuts or cobnuts

For leafy greens Instead of kale, use broccoli, spinach, rainbow chard or cavolo nero

We're bombarded by information and advertising all the time about super foods. For example, we're told that we need to consume more antioxidants, but did you know that antioxidants are happy with the pH level in the stomach, but not in the large intestine – which means that only about 1% of them can actually get into the blood stream. So perhaps we shouldn't be obsessing over them after all. It's so hard to know what to believe!

I'm not proclaiming that I know the secret to your health, beauty and eventual metamorphosis into Aphrodite (you need a different book for that). However, what I do know is that companies making wild, unproven claims about the purported health benefits of certain foods is rife, and the protective legislation we have in this area is lacking. In my opinion, governments should step in to make this false advertising illegal, for the sake of both our health and the unnecessary over farming of super not-so-super foods.

Sunflower Seed Butter

Have this on hot toast to kick-start your day with some omega-3s and protein. You can experiment with using all sorts of different seeds like pumpkin seeds or linseeds, and finding your own favourite variations and combinations. You can also try out this method using different nuts to make nut butter.

MAKES ABOUT 350 G/12⅓ OZ

250 G/9 OZ/1¾ CUPS RAW SUNFLOWER SEEDS

GOOD DRIZZLE OF OIL, SOMETHING BLAND LIKE SUNFLOWER WORKS BEST

SALT

Preheat the oven to 180°C fan/200°C/400°F/gas mark 6.

Spread the seeds out on a baking sheet and roast for about 3–4 minutes in a hot oven, just to colour slightly.

Pour the hot sunflower seeds into a food processor with a strong motor and blend – this bit will take a bit of time. They'll turn into a fine powder first, then become crumbly, then eventually smooth like peanut butter. You might need to use a spoon to scrape down the sides of the processor from time to time as you blend.

When you have reached the desired smooth texture, add oil and salt to taste, and blitz again until you have the perfect spreadable butter. Store the butter in the fridge for up to 3 months.

TIP

This would also make a great variation on a satay sauce – simply add 3 tbsp of the seed butter to a saucepan with 1 finely diced onion, 6 finely diced garlic cloves, 1 finely chopped red chilli, 1 tbsp soy sauce or Mushroom Ketchup (page 64), 1 tbsp caster (superfine) sugar and 1 can of coconut milk. Bring to the boil, then simmer for 5 minutes until slightly thickened and use as you need.

17

FAT

This is possibly one of the trickiest subjects to talk about. We have so much fear about fat that conjures up awful connotations and Armageddon conclusions. But to shine a ray of sunny hope over the subject, do you remember the chapter on fish, and how important omega-3 fatty acids are for our brain and health? Well, it turns out that fats can be great for us.

Yes, too much fat in the body is not good for you. Yes, there are some unhealthy fats, trans fats being the worst. And yes, excessive amounts of carbohydrates and protein can also turn into body fat!

But fat is also great. Fat is a source of the essential fatty acids that our bodies can't make themselves, which help us to absorb vitamins A, D and E. There is still so much research to be done to draw really conclusive results about the health effects of fat, but one thing we know is that we should be eating a varied diet with a range of fats, focusing primarily on monounsaturated and polyunsaturated fats.

But how can a fat be sustainable?

One of the most important points to note about food sustainability is that monoculture has negative effects on the environment as well as the food it's making for us. Coconut oil is supposed to be a super food, but if it's grown badly, sprayed with chemicals and causes deforestation and destruction, then I don't think it's all that super. If the whole world decides that coconut oil is the only fat to eat, then this is really detrimental both to the environment and to the quality of coconut oil. Diversity and quality are the keys to our survival and how good our food tastes.

Sustainable fats should follow the same key principles outlined in this book: zero waste, organic and 50% sourced within 30 miles. One easy way to eat a varied diet of fats is to vary your cooking techniques, switching between grilling, baking, steaming, boiling, roasting or poaching your foods.

A world without fat

Fat makes food taste great. We can't deny it, I'm afraid. It's a chemical reaction in our bodies – we know it's an instant source of energy that we can store. Nowadays food is available everywhere, and we probably don't need to store fat away for those long, cold winters.

My wife was brought up as a vegetarian, so naturally when we got together I had to adapt my cooking. This also came at a funny time, just as my dad was starting up a butcher's and cured meat company. What my wife taught me was that vegetables need love and attention – cooking red onions and peppers slowly brings out their natural sweetness, whereas a salad needs to be as fresh as possible with a marvellous dressing.

One of the issues with vegetarian cooking is that there isn't a lot of fat in vegetables. Meat and fish already contain amazing fats that make them taste delicious and are an instant source of protein, fat and energy. So, what do we need to do to get the same results with vegetables? We need to somehow pair them with a fat to bring out their best flavours, which is why carrots basted in butter or tomatoes drizzled in olive oil or cheese melted over a jacket potato tastes so good. My recipes for flavoured butters and mayonnaises (pages 97–98) allow for just this.

Fat used in the right way can be healthy, sustainable and delicious. Like a glass of red wine. Drink responsibly. Eat fat responsibly.

Grass-fed butter

You are what you're eating is eating... and so on. Basically, if your cows are eating grass all the time then, in theory, the butter made from their milk should be a very good source of vitamin A, omega-3s and, more importantly, vitamin K, which helps to keep calcium out of our arteries. Butter is around two-thirds saturated fat and one-third polyunsaturated fat, so it does contain good fats. Around three tablespoons a day is supposedly a good amount to eat. Despite what anyone says about butter, buy organic and grass-fed, not only for the best taste but also as the most sustainable option.

Now you might say I can't find organic and grass-fed in my supermarkets... well demand it! You have the power. Supermarkets stock what you want; they are driven by demand, so demand grass-fed butter, demand a better world and demand a healthier you.

The more natural the fat, the better it is for the earth and for you. Loving the planet means loving yourself.

Cooking with fats

When using oils that have a lower smoking point, it forces us to cook more slowly, helping us to bring out the best flavours. Imagine you're an Italian nonna taking her time over a pot of something delicious for the family.

High smoking points – high heat cooking Rapeseed oil, sunflower oil, ghee, nut oils, corn oil, beef dripping, coconut oil

Lower smoking points – sauté foods and slow cooking Extra virgin olive oil, lard, butter

Sage Butter

MAKES 250 G/9 OZ

3 GARLIC CLOVES, GRATED

1 LARGE BUNCH OF FRESH SAGE, FINELY DICED

250 G/9 OZ/2¼ STICKS SALTED BUTTER, AT ROOM TEMPERATURE

Put all the ingredients into a food processor and blitz for 30 seconds. The butter can be stored in ramekins in the fridge or ice trays in the freezer.

Café de Paris Butter

MAKES 250 G/9 OZ

3 ANCHOVIES, FINELY DICED

3 GARLIC CLOVES, FINELY DICED

HANDFUL OF FRESH PARSLEY, FINELY DICED

1 TBSP PINK PEPPERCORNS

1 TBSP FRESH THYME LEAVES, FINELY DICED

1 TSP CHILLI FLAKES (HOT RED PEPPER FLAKES)

FINELY GRATED ZEST OF 1 LEMON

1 TBSP MUSTARD

2 TBSP HOMEMADE WORCESTERSHIRE SAUCE (PAGE 84)

250 G/9 OZ/2¼ STICKS SALTED BUTTER, AT ROOM TEMPERATURE

Add all the ingredients to a food processor and blend together until combined.

The butter can be stored in ramekins in the fridge or ice trays in the freezer.

Harissa Butter

MAKES 250 G/9 OZ

10 RED CHILLIES

OIL OF YOUR CHOICE, FOR DRIZZLING

1 TSP GROUND CUMIN

1 TSP GROUND CORIANDER

1 TSP FENNEL SEEDS

250 G/9 OZ/2¼ STICKS SALTED BUTTER, AT ROOM TEMPERATURE

Preheat the oven to 160°C fan/180°C/350°F/gas mark 4.

Place the chillies on a baking sheet and drizzle with a little oil. Roast them in the oven for 10 minutes, then sprinkle over the spices and roast for a further 5 minutes. Remove from the oven and leave to cool slightly.

Add the roasted chillies to a food processor and blend for about a minute, then add the butter and blitz for another 30 seconds. The butter can be stored in ramekins in the fridge or ice trays in the freezer.

Beetroot Mayonnaise

Tarragon Aioli

MAKES ABOUT 500 ML/17 FL OZ/2 CUPS

1 RAW RED BEETROOT, UNPEELED
3 EGG YOLKS
1 TBSP MUSTARD
3 TBSP VINEGAR OF YOUR CHOICE
400 ML/14 FL OZ/1¾ CUPS OIL OF YOUR CHOICE
SALT
LEMON JUICE (OPTIONAL)

MAKES ABOUT 500 ML/17 FL OZ/2 CUPS

3 EGG YOLKS
BUNCH OF FRESH TARRAGON LEAVES
1 TBSP MUSTARD
5 GARLIC CLOVES, GRATED
3 TBSP VINEGAR OF YOUR CHOICE
500 ML/17 FL OZ/2 CUPS OIL OF YOUR CHOICE
SALT
LEMON JUICE (OPTIONAL)

Preheat the oven to 180°C fan/200°C/400°F/gas mark 6.

Put the whole beetroot in a baking dish and roast in the oven for 45 minutes. After cooking, let it cool and peel the skin off (this is for the compost). Cut the beetroot into quarters and add it to a food processor. Add the egg yolks, the mustard and the vinegar. Turn the food processor on and slowly add the oil, starting with drips and building up to a steady trickle, until blended and combined into a smooth mayo. Season the mayo with salt and add more vinegar or lemon juice to taste.

Put the egg yolks, tarragon leaves, mustard, grated garlic and the vinegar in a food processor. Turn the food processor on and slowly add the oil, starting with drips and building up to a steady trickle, until blended and combined into a smooth aioli. Season the aioli with salt and add more vinegar or lemon juice to taste.

Warm Wild Garlic Sauce

MAKES ABOUT 350 ML/12 FL OZ/1½ CUPS

3 EGG YOLKS

LARGE BUNCH OF WILD GARLIC (RAMPS)

1 TBSP MUSTARD

3 TBSP VINEGAR OF YOUR CHOICE

300 ML/10 FL OZ/1¼ CUPS MILD TASTING COLD-PRESSED OIL, SUCH AS SUNFLOWER

SALT

Put the egg yolks, wild garlic, mustard and vinegar in a food processor. Turn the food processor on and slowly add the oil, starting with drips and building up to a steady trickle, until blended and combined into a smooth mayonnaise. Season with salt and add more vinegar to taste.

For every two people, place 4 tablespoons of the mayonnaise in a small saucepan. Add 8 tablespoons of water and slowly bring up to a medium heat (not too high or it will curdle). Stir the sauce as it warms through and season again to taste, if needed, before serving.

Anchoïade

Why is it that when we translate something into French it suddenly sounds very appealing - like *jus d'agneau* instead of lamb juices, or *croque monsieur* instead of a cheese and ham toastie. Anchoïade is just a really fancy name for an anchovy dip, despite that it packs a punch and guarantees a flavoursome accompaniment for any moment.

12 ANCHOVY FILLETS, DRAINED IF IN OIL, RINSED IF SALTED, ROUGHLY CHOPPED

3 GARLIC CLOVES, ROUGHLY CHOPPED

SMALL BUNCH OF FRESH BASIL, STALKS ONLY, KEEP THE LEAVES FOR SOMETHING ELSE

SMALL BUNCH OF FRESH PARSLEY, STALKS ONLY, KEEP THE LEAVES FOR SOMETHING ELSE

1 TSP DRIED OREGANO

1 TBSP VINEGAR OF YOUR CHOICE

150 ML/5 FL OZ/⅔ CUP COLD-PRESSED OIL OF YOUR CHOICE

Put the all the ingredients, apart from the oil, in a food processor and blitz. Scrape down the sides, then pour in the oil slowly with the motor running. Scrape the sides again if needed and blitz again until well combined and smooth. Serve on toast with goat's cheese, or as a dip with the freshest and crunchiest garden vegetables.

GLUTEN

18

Gluten is not evil. There, I've said it... it's not evil. Just like all food is not evil, but, if we eat too much sugar, it can give us diabetes, and too many bananas can give us potassium overdose and too much kale can lead to poor absorption of nutrients and dehydration. Too much of anything is the problem.

But it's not just the quantity of what we eat, it's all about the quality of the food that we eat. Gluten has changed so much over the last 60 years. Traditionally, bread was always made using slow-rising yeast, allowing the gluten proteins to be broken down. Sourdough was a natural evolution and a way of life, not a luxury choice. And as a result, it contains lots of minerals like B-vitamins, zinc, copper, iron, magnesium and that all-important fibre. The great thing about fibre is that it allows us to release sugar energy slowly whilst also feeling full.

Ancient grains like spelt, emmer, einkorn and khorasan are delicious whole grains with loads of great nutrients that can be made into bread. They are slightly more difficult to work with and might need a bit more kneading to work the gluten more, but the results are worth it. People who are gluten sensitive could probably stick to varieties like einkorn or sourdough and not feel bloated or tired. Coeliac disease, however, is a different matter and any form of gluten should be avoided.

Nowadays, we are able to separate the nutritious components of the grain from the endosperm, where most of the starchy carbohydrates are contained. This has led to a market of wheat products with very low nutrient density, which have the ability to spike blood sugar very fast. A common reason that most people feel better when they go gluten free is because they're giving up processed foods first, including the spongy white bread that makes fish finger sandwiches taste so good!

The more we know about what goes into our foods, either at home or eating out, the safer and healthier we will be. These days, we can find all sorts of fantastic gluten-free flours like fava bean (broad bean), pea, buckwheat, chickpea and millet. We should all experiment with using them and reduce the amount of gluten we're eating. There are so many delicious options – how about sweetcorn fritters with broad bean (fava bean) flour, or broccoli bhajis using pea flour, or buckwheat pancakes like they enjoy in northern France?

The more creative we get, the tastier, healthier and more sustainable our food is. The more sustainable your food, the less likely it is that you'll have an intolerance to it. So let's go for it again... gluten is not evil. Rather, it is the magic elasticity that makes things stick together in high heat situations like wood-fired ovens. Gluten is the science that allows yeast to do the hard work for us. Let's use it to our advantage and slow down our lives and slow down our rising yeasts!

Omega-3 Slow-rise Spelt Seeded Bread

Slow-rise bread is super delicious. It tastes so good because the flavour is allowed more time to develop as the yeast performs its vital role converting sugars to carbon dioxide and alcohol. Whilst this is happening, enzymes in the flour also slowly break down the gluten proteins into smaller pieces, making it easier to digest. If you are out at work during the day, then this recipe is perfect - make the dough in the morning and leave to prove, then when you return knock back and do the second knead and prove before baking.

MAKES 1 LOAF

500 G/1 LB 2 OZ/5 CUPS SPELT FLOUR, PLUS EXTRA FOR THE WORK SURFACE

2 TBSP SALT

50 G/1¾ OZ SEEDS (SUNFLOWER, PUMPKIN OR LINSEED)

15 G/½ OZ FRESH YEAST OR 8 G/¼ OZ DRIED INSTANT YEAST

330 ML/11 FL OZ/1⅓ CUPS COLD WATER

EQUIPMENT
25-CM/10-INCH LOAF PAN

Mix the flour, salt and seeds together in a large mixing bowl. In a separate bowl, add the yeast to the cold water and mix until dissolved using your hands. Mix the yeast-water into the flour. Bring the mixture together into a dough using your hands. Turn out onto a lightly floured work surface and knead for 10 minutes.

Place the dough back in the bowl, cover with a clean kitchen cloth and leave to slowly prove at room temperature (not too warm) for about 8–10 hours until doubled in size.

Preheat the oven at 200°C fan/220°C/425°F/gas mark 7.

Turn the dough out onto the work surface and knock back by kneading through again for 5 minutes. Shape into a loaf, place in the loaf pan and leave to prove again in a warm area until the dough has risen above the top of the pan.

Bake in the oven for 30 minutes, or until the loaf sounds hollow when tapped. Take the loaf out of the pan and leave to cool on a cooling rack before slicing and eating.

Soda Bread

My wife Lauren and I spent a holiday travelling the west coast of Ireland and it is quite possibly the humblest and most beautiful place on earth - wild, raw, energetic, simple and powerful - just like the food. Soda bread is simple, delicious and full of life. It is half bread, half cake and has the best qualities of both. There is nothing better than warm soda bread with rich, salty butter. A simple act of baking over the weekend will mean you can enjoy the spoils throughout the week (or slice and freeze some if you wish) with the full knowledge that your homemade bread has left no transportation carbon footprint. A little locally milled flour, some milk and vinegar are all you need to create this most excellent of breads. Add an Irish chowder, an Irish stout and an extraordinary sea view into the equation and you're a lucky person.

MAKES 1 LOAF

2 TBSP CIDER VINEGAR

400ML/14FL OZ/1¾ CUPS MILK

250G/9OZ/2 CUPS PLAIN (ALL-PURPOSE) FLOUR, PLUS EXTRA FOR THE WORK SURFACE

250G/9OZ/SCANT 2 CUPS WHOLEMEAL FLOUR

1 TSP SALT

1 TSP BICARBONATE OF SODA

To make buttermilk, add the vinegar to the milk and stir until well combined. Leave to stand for 10 minutes. Meanwhile, preheat your oven to 200°C fan/220°C/425°F/gas mark 7. Mix the flours, salt and bicarbonate together. Add about three quarters of the buttermilk gradually and mix thoroughly to form a sticky dough. You may not need to add all the buttermilk as this could make the dough too wet – it really depends on the absorbency of the flour.

Knead the dough for a few minutes, then turn out onto a floured work surface and shape into a ball. Transfer to a baking sheet, score the top into quarters with a sharp knife, flour lightly and bake for 30 minutes or until the loaf sounds hollow when tapped.

A LITTLE NOTE ON ORGANIC CULTURE...

Organic culture is diversity – it is an expression of the land, it is the opposite of predictability, monoculture and GMOs – and it is very evident in flour! Each year we have to buy the new season's flour, made from that year's wheat grown in the neighbouring fields, and each year we have to change the recipe a little for pizzas because each year's wheat has a different composition of water and protein, which in turn will affect the recipe.

Broad Bean Flatbreads with Black Onion Seeds

I think one of the most exciting things about the sustainable cooking movement is the variety of new dishes and flavours that will come out of it. Broad bean flour is simply dried broad (fava) beans that have been ground into a powder. And, to be honest, you can use this recipe as an opportunity to try out all sorts of flour alternatives here such as marrowfat pea flour, yellow pea flour, buckwheat flour, rye flour, quinoa flour or maslin flour. Just remember that they will all absorb water slightly differently, so you may need to add a little more or less. The batter consistency should be like thick double (heavy) cream.

MAKES ABOUT 4 FLATBREADS

150 G/5½ OZ/GENEROUS 1 CUP BROAD BEAN (FAVA BEAN) FLOUR

PINCH OF SALT

OIL OF YOUR CHOICE, FOR FRYING

BLACK ONION SEEDS

Mix the flour and salt together with 250 ml/8½ fl oz/generous 1 cup water in a mixing bowl. Leave to sit for 10 minutes.

Put some oil in a frying pan (skillet) over a medium heat. Add 2–3 large spoonfuls of the mixture to the hot pan and use the back of the spoon to gently move the batter around in a circular motion and increase the size to about 8 cm/3 inches in diameter. Repeat for 1–2 more flatbreads, depending on the size of your pan. Sprinkle a generous pinch of black onion seeds over each flatbread on the side that isn't cooking while they are still wet.

After 3–5 minutes, the bottoms should be cooked and golden. Flip the flatbreads and cook for a further 3 minutes on the other side.

Serve with a curry or perhaps a spiced baked bean breakfast.

Oat Pancakes

Large oats are a fantastic source of energy, nutrients and flavour. Plus they're grown all over the UK and very locally to me, so I wanted to find a way to use them without resorting to porridge all the time. These little pancakes can be served as a savoury breakfast with fried eggs or as a sweet one with berries, yogurt and honey. At the pub we actually serve them as an appetizer, often with chargrilled mackerel and a pickled fennel salad.

SERVES 2 (MAKES 4 PANCAKES)

200 G/7 OZ/2 GENEROUS CUPS ROLLED OATS

200 ML/6¾ FL OZ/GENEROUS ¾ CUP MILK OF YOUR CHOICE (OR USE WATER IF YOU WANT)

2 EGGS

PINCH OF SALT

50 G/1¾ OZ/½ CUP JUMBO OATS

SALTED BUTTER OR BLAND OIL, FOR FRYING

Blend the rolled oats to the texture of flour in a food processor. Put the oat flour in a bowl and whisk with the milk, eggs, pinch of salt and jumbo oats and leave to rest for 15 minutes.

Put a frying pan (skillet) over a medium heat with either some butter or bland oil. Dollop a large tablespoonful of pancake mixture into the pan and fry for 2–3 minutes until golden and crisp underneath, flip over and cook the other side until golden again. Serve. I like to do two each because I'm greedy.

19 DAIRY

The truth is out: we need to reduce the amount of dairy that we are consuming. Cow husbandry is one of the largest contributors to global warming and deforestation, and it also uses huge amounts of water, food and energy.

This doesn't necessarily mean that we should all jump ship and drink alternatives to milk. Milk alternatives do not naturally have the same micronutrients as cow's milk – and if the cow is grown organically and grass fed, then its dairy will contain some wonderful nutrients for us. Alternatives and substitutes to dairy can still be highly processed products that may have been sprayed with pesticides, may cause mass deforestation and make huge water losses. The aim is to consume better produce – using animals that have been reared organically, that are local and grass fed. And, of course, in order to reduce the amount of dairy consumed overall, we should also supplement with sustainable alternatives.

You can find any article on the internet these days to justify the argument you're making – the facts are that everyone is unique and reacts differently to different foods, so you need to find what works best for you. Historically lots of cultures had evolved to eat dairy because otherwise they would have starved. Nowadays, we just don't need it as much. If you're worried about where your calcium will come from if you eat less dairy, calcium can also come in other forms like green vegetables, nuts, soya and fish where we eat the bones, like sardines.

It's also important to mention that herding animals for dairy in a responsible way can be good for the ecosystems of the planet. Grazing animals is one of the best ways to solve desertification, and can return arid areas of land to lush greenery, which in turn helps to turn CO_2 back into oxygen. We have an amazing symbiotic relationship with animals, and we should value that.

Sustainability is the best diet for you and for the earth.

TIP!
Local alternatives to cow's milk
Both goat's milk and ewe's milk contain smaller lactose globules – not only is this a really funny phrase, but it also means that their milk is easier to digest. Give them a go. Both milks can be very local and very delicious.

Omega-3 Butters

If you want to reduce the amount of dairy butter you eat or increase the amount of omega-3s, then these two recipes work well. I tend to just use them for spreading on toast or for melting and drizzling over vegetables.

Option 1

Put 250 g/9 oz/2¼ sticks soft salted butter in a food processor, turn on, then slowly drizzle in 250 ml/8½ fl oz/generous 1 cup of a cold-pressed oil of your choice – rapeseed or olive are nice.

Option 2

Frozen mayonnaise works as a butter replacement as well – slowly combine 2 egg yolks with 500 ml/17 fl oz/2 cups of a bland cold-pressed oil in a food processor. Place in a covered container in the freezer ready for use. (Eggs are the best natural emulsifier, you don't need to resort to the more processed 'spreads' found in supermarkets.)

Homemade Cheat's Ricotta

This cheat's ricotta is simply curds separated from whey. Almost all cheese making involves this basic process in one form or another. You will be left with the whey, which is itself an amazing product - slightly sweet, very nutritious and a great stock for soups or sauces or addition to your smoothie or morning porridge.

MAKES 500 G/1 LB 2 OZ

2 LITRES/3½ PINTS/GENEROUS 8½ CUPS WHOLE MILK
1 TSP SALT
1 TSP CITRIC ACID

EQUIPMENT
COOKING THERMOMETER
RICOTTA MOULDS OR A SIEVE (STRAINER)

Place the milk and salt in a large saucepan and slowly bring the mixture up to 93°C/199°F, measuring with a cooking thermometer and stirring frequently. When the temperature is reached, turn off the heat, stir in the citric acid and allow to set for 30 minutes without stirring.

Using a slotted spoon, carefully remove the set curds and place into ricotta moulds or a sieve (strainer). If using a sieve, drain for 2 minutes and then transfer to a container. Refrigerate the curds for at least 2 hours before using or until needed for up to 2 days.

The leftover whey should be kept in a container in the fridge or used to make a béchamel sauce.

Courgette, Pea, and Cobnut Salad with Homemade Ricotta

Another summer classic, this time green and fresh. Other than the well-known five tastes, salty, sweet, sour, acidic and umami, I think there's another flavour - freshness. The mouth knows how fresh the produce is, it has an alive sensation as well as feeling lush and moist. Use the freshest possible vegetables you can find in this dish for their great crunchy textures (page 111).

SERVES 2

SALT

200 G/7 OZ FRESH PEAS OR MANGETOUT (SNOW PEAS) OR BROAD BEANS (FAVA BEANS) OR A MIXTURE OF ALL THREE

3 COURGETTES (ZUCCHINI), SHAVED INTO RIBBONS WITH A PEELER

100 G/3½ OZ ROCKET (ARUGULA)

HANDFUL OF COBNUTS OR OTHER LOCALLY SOURCED NUTS, ROUGHLY CHOPPED

SMALL HANDFUL OF FRESH MINT, ROUGHLY CHOPPED

200 G/7 OZ HOMEMADE CHEAT'S RICOTTA (SEE LEFT)

EDIBLE FLOWERS, TO GARNISH (OPTIONAL)

FOR THE DRESSING

4 TBSP CIDER VINEGAR

1 TBSP HONEY

PINCH OF SALT

12 TBSP COLD-PRESSED OIL OF YOUR CHOICE

Bring a large pan of salted water to the boil. When boiling, add the peas, mangetout or broad beans. Boil for 1 minute, then immediately transfer the vegetables to a bowl of iced water for 1 minute before draining well.

Place the courgette ribbons, rocket, chopped nuts and mint in a large mixing bowl with your cooked vegetables. Whisk the vinegar, honey, salt and oil together in a small bowl for the dressing. Drizzle some of the dressing over the salad and mix together gently.

Mound the salad onto serving plates and nestle blobs of your Homemade Cheat's Ricotta over. Finish with a drizzle of the dressing and serve garnished with edible flowers if you like.

Oat Milk

Chocolate Sorbet

Going along with the ethos of this chapter and using produce within 30 miles, oats are grown in many areas of England, India, Australia and around the world and contain many delicious nutrients.

This recipe is so easy, and so deliciously creamy that no-one can believe it's dairy free!

MAKES 1 LITRE/1¾ PINTS/4 CUPS

MAKES 2 LITRES/3½ PINTS/GENEROUS 8½ CUPS

400 G/14 OZ/2 CUPS GOLDEN CASTER (SUPERFINE) SUGAR

150 G/5½ OZ/1½ CUPS COCOA POWDER

400 G/14 OZ DARK (BITTERSWEET) CHOCOLATE, BROKEN INTO PIECES

EQUIPMENT

ICE CREAM MACHINE

Soak the oats in 1 litre/1¾ pints/4 cups water for at least an hour, then drain and rinse the oats under running water. Now blend the oats in a food processor with 800 ml/1½ pints/3⅓ cups fresh water until completely blended into a liquid. Strain the milk through a cheesecloth (muslin) or sieve (strainer). Bottle and store the oat milk in the fridge for up to 3 days.

Put the sugar and cocoa powder in a saucepan with 1 litre/1¾ pints/4 cups water and bring to a simmer, whisking to incorporate.

Pour the hot cocoa syrup over the broken chocolate in a bowl and whisk vigorously until smooth and combined. Leave to cool, then transfer to an ice cream machine and churn following the manufacturer's instructions.

TIP

After straining the oats, you'll be left with the by-product of oat fibre, which is incredibly nutritious and helps to digest certain nutrients properly. Instead of discarding the oats, use them in a batch of flapjacks or blend with fruits for your morning smoothie.

CHIPS

CHOC BAR

We all love to snack – while watching a film, with a cup of tea, dinner party nibbles, that mid-morning twitch, and sometimes we just get a little rumble in the jungle (growl from the stomach). We want our snacks to be rewarding, tasty and satisfying.

But snacking is one of the easiest ways to eat too much sugar or fill up on low-nutrient carbs.

Large companies pay scientists huge sums of money to create snacks that have 'the bliss point' – that special mixture of enough fat, salt and sugar to make us want more and more and more.

Learn what your personal bliss point is so that you can make your own more nutritious, moreish and sustainable snacks.

Crispy Deep-fried Broad Beans

I have nightmares about overly soft, tasteless broad beans in white sauce, something left over from the 80s probably. But if they're used properly, they can be gems of delight with a great texture that you don't get with its cousin, the pea. What I love about beans is that they can be dried and stored for the months to come - they really are one of the great staples that helped us survive those difficult months when nothing grew. We should actually treat them with a lot more respect than to smother them in generic white sauce. Good riddance. Here I'm using them as a snack. Delicious, nutritious and good for the soil and bees, broad beans are Britain's original bean, grown here since the Iron Age.

SERVES 3–4 AS A SNACK

300 G/10½ OZ/1¾ CUPS DRIED SPLIT BROAD BEANS (FAVA BEANS)

OIL WITH A HIGH SMOKING POINT, SUCH AS RAPESEED OR SUNFLOWER, FOR DEEP-FRYING

6 TBSP FLOUR - BROAD (FAVA) BEAN FLOUR HAS A GREAT TASTE, BUT CHICKPEA (GRAM) FLOUR OR PLAIN FOUR WORK JUST AS WELL

FLAVOURED SALT OF YOUR CHOICE (PAGE 22)

Soak the beans for at least 8 hours or overnight in lots of cold water.

If you have an electric deep-fryer, turn it to 180°C/350°F. If you don't have one, then find a very deep heavy-bottomed pan and fill with 5 cm/ 2 inches of oil. Heat the oil to 180°C/350°F using a cooking thermometer, or until a cube of bread browns in 30 seconds.

Drain the soaked beans well and toss them in the flour. Deep-fry them in batches for a minute or two until crispy. Remove with a slotted spoon and drain any excess oil. Place on a tray and sprinkle with your favourite flavoured salt. These are best eaten when fresh and crispy but you can store the beans in an airtight container for about a week.

MAKE YOUR FAVOURITE MEAL CHALLENGE

Congratulations, you're well on your way to becoming a sustainable food ambassador. It's not too hard is it? And I hope you've eaten some tasty food so far. This next step is all about creating your favourite meal but making it as sustainable as you possibly can – I'm sure it'll actually be easier than you think. Ask friends, look on websites, visit independent shops, be curious and adventure into making your favourite meal even more rewarding than before.

First challenge

Think about reducing your waste – no single-use plastic.

Second challenge

Buy organic as much as possible. But don't rebuy expensive items like spices if you already have them.

Third challenge

Are all your vegetables or produce in season and produced within 30 miles? If not, is there an alternative that's local? If you need to buy imported produce can you make up for it somewhere else?

If you need meat, look for grass fed and organic or think about buying the whole animal, if it's chicken, for example. Make everything yourself – if you love pies then make your own pastry using local, organic and sustainable flour and fat. If it's pizza you love, then make your own dough using organic flour, find some local cheeses and see what toppings you make yourself. If you're buying fish, go to a fishmonger and ask how it was caught and where it was from. For grains or pulses, try to use local varieties – check the comparison chart on page 141 to find what you can replace rice with, for example. If it's pasta, try and make it yourself with organic flour and organic eggs.

Once you've won the challenge, cooked and eaten your sustainable meal, and felt great doing it, continue reading because it's only going to get easier, better and tastier.

Scrambled Eggs

Now I know you think this might be me copping out of a challenge, but I would rather be honest. If there was one meal I could choose to eat before I die, it would be scrambled eggs. There is nothing more simple, yet more utterly perfect to me than scrambled eggs on toast. It was the only meal I would eat if I was ill as a child, it's still my favourite breakfast and my favourite dinner as well. It's the first thing I teach all chefs at the pub because if you can respect how to cook an egg you can respect all other ingredients. This technique does not need any butter or milk because it's all about letting the eggs shine.

So, my personal challenge here is to find the most organic and local eggs I can. Perhaps I should try keeping chickens? And then make my own bread using organic local flour, with seeds for added omega-3s. And where do I get my butter for the toast from? Is it from grass-fed organic cows, and perhaps I blend half butter with half cold-pressed oil for added unsaturated fats. Even within this simple dish, I'm asking myself questions, which lead to solutions and a healthier, tastier and more sustainable life.

SERVES 1

3 EGGS (YOU WANT 2 EGGS PER PERSON PLUS 1 EXTRA EGG)

SALT, TO TASTE

HOT BUTTERED TOAST, TO SERVE

Your only job is to look after these eggs – get someone else to make the tea, butter the toast, whatever – your only responsibility on earth right now is to not overcook these eggs.

Put the eggs in a cold pan and whisk together. Don't season yet, it'll split the whites from the yolks. Turn the hob (stove) to low–medium and start to cook your eggs. Constantly move the eggs around with a spoon, stirring and scraping the bottom of the pan as they cook. After a few minutes, you'll begin to feel them thicken. Don't be tempted to turn up the heat – if your pan is too hot it will over-scramble the eggs before you've had a chance to get them to the table. Continue to nurture the eggs, taking them off the heat every now and again so you have control over the temperature, and constantly folding them in on themselves. Let them thicken slowly – the whole process should take roughly 8 minutes. The pan shouldn't be too hot and the eggs should stop cooking as soon as you take the pan off the heat.

At this point your friend/partner/sous chef should put the buttered toast in front of you so that you can finally season the eggs with a little salt and spoon them over the toast. The consistency of perfectly cooked scrambled eggs should have its own scientific name, somewhere between wet, soft, solid, liquid, creamy, mushy and oozy. Above all, they should be bright yellow and seasoned perfectly.

WE NEED FLIES TO HAVE LIONS

What does this even mean? Crazy man... bet you never thought someone would ever talk about flies in a cookbook! What I mean is that every organism on earth is here because it has come out of evolution, i.e. the reason that we even have lions is because the flies were here before them.

Flies belong to a base layer of insects that help to connect the circle of life – they lay eggs on dead animals, which turn into larvae, that then eat the animal, decomposing it back into the essential nutrients for the ecosystem, starting the whole circle over again.

It's important to appreciate this because if humans start playing around with certain layers in the animal hierarchy pyramid, then we could make the whole thing tumble. We know already how fragile the bees are. People are proposing that we eat insects – my thoughts are if humans try to control the base layers of the pyramid, it could cause serious problems. Let's promote growth from the roots up.

We need large animals and small animals. We need large plants and small ones. Just as humans are all born equal, so all organisms on earth are too.

TROPHIC PYRAMID

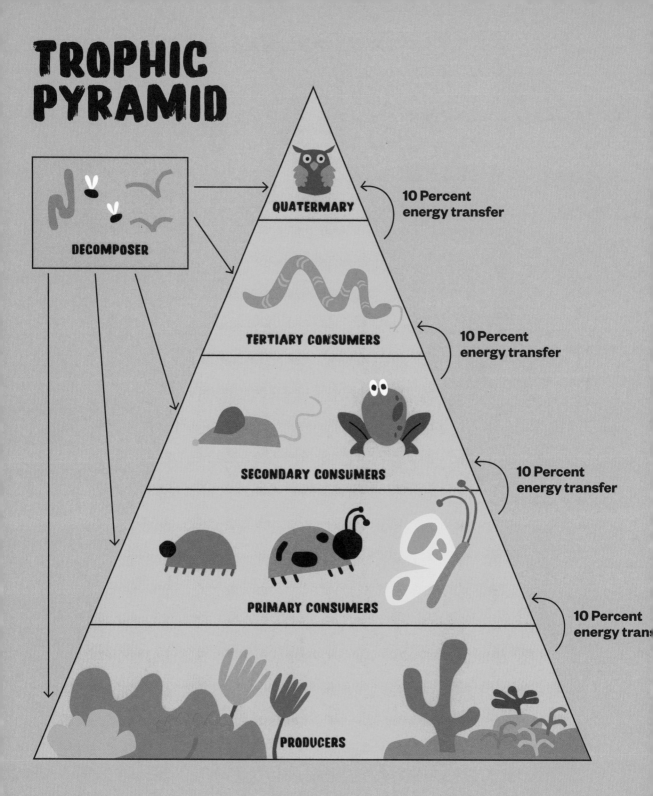

DECOMPOSER

QUATERMARY

10 Percent
energy transfer

TERTIARY CONSUMERS

10 Percent
energy transfer

SECONDARY CONSUMERS

10 Percent
energy transfer

PRIMARY CONSUMERS

10 Percent
energy trans

PRODUCERS

We Need Flies to Have Lions

Courgette Spread with Asparagus and a Flower Power Salad

This recipe is all about the flowers. Flowers give pollinators food and insects homes. By creating a demand for more flowers with recipes like this, we should have more flowers for our wonderful insects to enjoy. The aim is for you to grow more plants so that you can replenish what you take. Each flower in this salad has its own scrummy taste, creating a unique myriad of flavours!

SERVES 4

FOR THE SPREAD

4 COURGETTES (ZUCCHINI), CUT INTO 2.5-CM/1-INCH SLICES

COLD-PRESSED OLIVE OIL, FOR DRIZZLING

2 GARLIC CLOVES

SMALL BUNCH OF FRESH CHIVES

½ LEMON

FOR THE SALAD

20 ASPARAGUS STEMS

200 G/7 OZ ROCKET (ARUGULA)

A FEW BORAGE FLOWERS

A FEW CHIVE FLOWERS

A FEW NASTURTIUM FLOWERS

A FEW DANDELION FLOWERS

SMALL HANDFUL OF FRESH DILL

A FEW PEA SHOOTS

A FEW MARIGOLD FLOWERS

PINCH OF SALT

½ LEMON

COLD-PRESSED OLIVE OIL, FOR DRIZZLING

Preheat the oven to 180°C fan/200°C/400°F/gas mark 6.

Start by making the spread. Put the courgette slices in a roasting pan, drizzle with oil and roast in the oven for 15 minutes. Leave to cool slightly.

Place the roasted courgettes in a food processor with the garlic and chives. Blitz until smooth, adding the juice of half the lemon and perhaps some more oil to create a smooth consistency. Set aside.

Bring a saucepan of salted water to the boil. Add the asparagus and blanch for a few minutes until bright green. Drain and run under very cold water to immediately cool. Leave the asparagus to drain well.

Start to arrange the salad on a large serving platter. Spread a layer of courgette spread on the bottom of the plate. Place all the salad ingredients (apart from the asparagus and reserving a few flowers) in a mixing bowl. Sprinkle with a little salt, a drizzle of oil and a squeeze of lemon juice from the other half of the lemon. Very carefully mix the salad with your hands and place on top of the courgette spread.

Arrange the blanched asparagus spears on top of the salad and drizzle with a little oil. Scatter over any reserved flowers and serve.

Rose Petal Jam

There is nothing more quintessentially English than roses - their fragrance permeates our gardens and hedges, and is always accompanied by the gentle humming of bees looking for nectar. The problem with roses is that they can lose their petals very quickly once they have bloomed, so instead of letting nature swallow them up, I like to make them into a jam. Remove the flower heads just at that turning point for optimum flavour and fragrance, making sure there are no creepy crawlies hiding. If you like Turkish Delight, then this rose petal jam will change your mornings, desserts and teas for the better.

MAKES ABOUT 2 LITRES/3½ PINTS

500 G/1 LB 2 OZ/2½ CUPS CASTER (SUPERFINE) SUGAR

500 G/1 LB 2 OZ ROSE PETALS FROM THE GARDEN, CLEANED

JUICE OF 2 LEMONS

1 TSP PECTIN

EQUIPMENT

STERILIZED JARS

Place the sugar in a large saucepan with 1 litre/1¾ pints/4 cups water and bring to a simmer. Add the rose petals, lemon juice and the pectin.

Keep stirring constantly while the liquid simmers for 20 minutes. Bring the pan to a rolling boil for a further 5 minutes, still stirring to stop it from catching on the bottom of the pan. To test if the jam is ready for setting, spoon some of the mixture onto a chilled plate; if it keeps its shape then it is ready. If it doesn't hold, then boil for 5 more minutes and test again.

Pour the mixture into sterilized jars and allow to cool before covering and refrigerating. It will keep for up to 6 months in the fridge.

23 THE HUNGRY GAP

Hungry gap away team

It does what it says on the tin – this is a small period in April and May when the UK's farms are looking very thin and there's not a lot growing ready for consumption. The winter vegetables start to 'bolt', stopping all leaf growth so they can flower and seed, whilst our spring crops are still coming through and are not ready to be picked or eaten.

So, how can we survive? Do we rely on importing during these months? Do we buy extortionately priced vegetables from afar? Do we plant more ourselves, becoming more reliant on our own gardens and the community? Do we eat less? After all, we store fat just for these times.

The hungry gap away team is our opportunity to really embrace the modern luxury of imported produce, things that don't have too much environmental damage like spices, dried fruits, sustainable nuts and certain grains. Spices are an amazing way to excite the palate, whilst still using local vegetables or produce.

Hungry gap home team

The English summer of 2018 was one of the best in my memory – beautiful sunshine day after day, week after week. We almost felt Continental, not having anything to complain about. The produce thrived if watered well and those autumn vegetables were even better. The pub was amazingly busy and everyone was happy.

However, there was one problem – the previous year's supply of potatoes was going to run out in the coming December, and I needed more for the following year, but because of the serious lack of rain my future potatoes were not growing, no matter how hard Pete at Westmill Organics watered them.

I'm now writing this in 2019 and the potatoes are in short supply and only just larger than golf balls - not ideal for chips, mash or anything really. We are so reliant on nature, we need it because we need to eat, and the hungry gap is scary. But through generations of passing down knowledge and techniques, we have overcome this for thousands of years by preserving and foraging. In more modern times we have also been able to import from all over the world, freeze food or store produce in cans for years at a time.

For the hungry gap home team we look to recipes that are going to fill us with delight as much as keep us alive. Relying on grains and pulses that we stored from last summer, meats and fish that we've cured, fruits preserved in Kilner/mason jars, pickles and chutneys that have been maturing for months. It's all about getting more out of less, which means full stomachs and smiley faces.

WHAT YOU CAN EAT IN THE HUNGRY GAP

- Purple sprouting broccoli
- Wild garlic (ramps)
- Rhubarb
- Spring greens
- Chard/rainbow chard
- Asparagus
- New potatoes
- Borlotti beans
- Broad beans (fava beans)
- Marrowfat peas
- Split peas
- Lentils

- Spelt
- Cannellini beans
- Wild garlic tagliatelle
- Purple sprouting stir-fries
- Asparagus Caesar salad
- Spring green spelt risotto
- Pork and split pea stew
- Chorizo and fava bean pie
- Marrowfat pea and rainbow chard soup
- Mackerel with cannellini beans and homemade paprika

Broad Bean Falafels

These beautiful falafels are soft on the inside and crisp on the outside. They are delicious served in warm pitta breads with yogurt, rose harissa, a fresh coriander salad, pickles and olives.

MAKES ABOUT 12 FALAFELS

300 G/10½ OZ DRIED SPLIT BROAD BEANS (FAVA BEANS)

1 ONION, ROUGHLY CHOPPED

4 GARLIC CLOVES

2 TBSP BROAD BEAN (FAVA BEAN) FLOUR OR ANY OTHER FLOUR

3 TSP GROUND CUMIN

3 TSP GROUND CORIANDER

1 TSP GROUND CAYENNE PEPPER

OIL WITH A HIGH SMOKING POINT, SUCH AS RAPESEED OR SUNFLOWER

TO SERVE

WARM PITTA BREADS

YOGURT

ROSE HARISSA

CORIANDER (CILANTRO) SALAD

PICKLES AND OLIVES

Soak the beans in plenty of water overnight or for at least 8 hours before using.

Drain the beans and add to a food processor with all the other ingredients (apart from the oil for frying) and blitz until the mixture resembles a coarse paste. If it's too wet, gradually add more flour 1 tablespoon at a time until it mostly holds together. Shape the mixture into balls the size of golf balls.

Preheat the oven to 180°C fan/200°C/400°F/gas mark 6.

Add a good 2.5-cm/1-inch layer of oil to a heavy-bottomed saucepan over a medium heat. Heat the oil to 180°C/350°F, or until a piece of the mixture sizzles and turns golden when dropped in. Carefully add about half the batch of falafel balls and deep-fry, turning regularly, until dark golden all over. Remove with a slotted spoon and drain any excess oil. Split one open to see if they are cooked on the inside – it should have changed colour to be bright yellow – if not then place the batch in the hot oven for a couple of minutes. Repeat the cooking process with any remaining falafel mixture and serve.

Fresh Tagliatelle with Wild Garlic Pesto and Rainbow Chard

This pasta recipe uses more eggs than normal which makes it rich and silky smooth - great for a treat. Nuts can be very expensive, so to keep with the thriftiness of foraging, using roasted seeds in the pesto is an excellent alternative way to create beautiful flavour without breaking the bank.

SERVES 4

FOR THE EGG PASTA

500 G/1 LB 2 OZ/4 SCANT CUPS ITALIAN '00' FLOUR, PLUS EXTRA FOR FLOURING YOUR HANDS AND DUSTING

15 G/½ OZ/3 TSP FINE SALT

2 TBSP OLIVE OIL

4 EGGS

4 EGG YOLKS

FOR THE WILD GARLIC PESTO

LARGE BUNCH OF WILD GARLIC (RAMPS)

LARGE BUNCH OF FRESH PARSLEY

100 G/3½ OZ/⅓-½ CUP ROASTED SUNFLOWER SEEDS

200 G/7 OZ HARD CHEESE, GRATED - I USE AGED WESTCOMBE CHEDDAR - PLUS EXTRA TO SERVE

OLIVE OIL

SALT

TO SERVE

200 G/7 OZ RAINBOW CHARD, SLICED

WILD GARLIC (RAMPS) FLOWERS

EQUIPMENT

PASTA MACHINE

PASTA RACK (IDEALLY) OR A CLEAN POLE

For the pasta, add the flour, salt, olive oil, eggs and egg yolks to a mixing bowl. Using your hands, break up and whisk the eggs and egg yolks, then mix the dough together. If your hands get too sticky, dust with flour.

Turn out the dough onto a clean work surface and knead lightly until bound together and silky smooth. Cut into equal quarters. (At this point you can put some of the dough in containers and freeze what you don't need or roll it all out and use the excess later in the week). Cover the dough with a cloth and let it rest for at least 30 minutes in the fridge.

Attach a pasta machine to a table. Flatten a piece of dough with your hands and run through the machine on the thickest setting. Dust with flour, take the thickness down a notch and run through the machine again. Repeat until you reach the second to last thickness (2 mm). If at any stage your dough gets a hole, fold it in half and run through the machine again. Repeat for the remaining dough.

Either cut the pasta into finger-width ribbons by hand with a sharp knife or use the pasta machine attachments to make the shape you want. If you have a pasta rack then leave the pasta to hang and dry in the fridge, which is the best way. Alternatively, you can leave it to hang and dry on a clean pole for 30 minutes, then store it lying down on a tray in the fridge covered with a clean kitchen cloth.

For the pesto, put the wild garlic, parsley, roasted seeds and grated cheese into a food processor and blitz. Scrape down the sides. Add enough olive oil to let the pesto down to the correct consistency – it should be oozy but not runny. Season with salt.

Bring a large pan of salted water to the boil. Drop the pasta in and simmer for a couple of minutes until al dente. Drain, reserving some of the pasta water and add the pasta back into the pan, with 1 large tablespoon of pesto per person, the rainbow chard and a half a ladle of pasta water. Mix together thoroughly to ensure the pasta is coated in sauce and cook over a medium heat until reduced and combined.

Serve with some more freshly grated cheese and garnish with some wild garlic flowers. Keep any leftover pesto in the fridge for up to 5 days.

Curried Halloumi, Cauliflower and Coconut Purée, Curried Almond Sauce

I actually made a similar dish to this on *MasterChef* which got me through to the semi-finals. Who doesn't love warming spices and vibrant colours on their plate?

SERVES 4

500 G/1 LB 2 OZ HALLOUMI

1 LARGE TBSP MEDIUM CURRY POWDER

OIL, FOR FRYING

SEEDS FROM 1 RIPE POMEGRANATE

CAULIFLOWER AND COCONUT PURÉE

1 ONION, ROUGHLY CHOPPED

3 GARLIC CLOVES, ROUGHLY CHOPPED

1 LARGE CAULIFLOWER, ROUGHLY CHOPPED AND LEAVES SET ASIDE

1 X 400-ML/14-FL OZ CAN COCONUT MILK

1 STAR ANISE

SALT

FOR THE CURRIED ALMOND SAUCE

1 ONION, ROUGHLY CHOPPED

3 GARLIC CLOVES, ROUGHLY CHOPPED

1 RED CHILLI

CHUNK OF FRESH GINGER, FINELY CHOPPED

BUNCH OF FRESH CORIANDER (CILANTRO), STALKS ROUGHLY CHOPPED AND LEAVES LEFT WHOLE

1 TSP GROUND TURMERIC

1 TSP GROUND CUMIN

1 TSP GROUND CORIANDER

100 G/3½ OZ/¾ CUP BLANCHED WHOLE ALMONDS

200 G/7 OZ/SCANT 1 CUP PLAIN YOGURT

½ LIME

Cut the halloumi into thick steaks and sprinkle with some curry powder on both sides. Set to one side.

For the cauliflower and coconut purée, put some glugs of oil in a saucepan over a medium heat. Add the chopped onion and garlic cloves and sauté until soft. Add the chopped cauliflower and can of coconut milk. Season with salt and add the star anise. Simmer for 5–10 minutes until the cauliflower is soft. Remove the star anise, then blend to a purée in a food processor. Set aside.

For the curried almond sauce, put some oil in a clean saucepan over a medium heat. Add the chopped onion, garlic, chilli, ginger and coriander stalks and sauté until soft. Add the ground turmeric, cumin and coriander and cook for 2 minutes. Add the blanched almonds, yogurt and 200 ml/6¾ fl oz/generous ¾ cup water. Bring to a gentle simmer and cook for 20 minutes. Remove from the heat and finish with a squeeze of lime. Transfer to a food processor and blitz to a smooth sauce. Set aside.

Preheat the grill (broiler) on a high setting.

Place the curried halloumi slices on a baking sheet and drizzle with a little oil. Grill (broil) the halloumi until each side is a deep golden colour.

When you are ready to serve, heat the cauliflower purée and curried almond sauce through in separate saucepans until warm. Ladle the curried almond sauce into the bottom of four shallow serving bowls, then spoon the cauliflower and coconut purée in the middle of each. Place the grilled curried halloumi slices on top. Finish the dishes with scatterings of fresh coriander leaves, pomegranate seeds and cauliflower leaves.

The Broad Bean Flatbreads with Black Onion Seeds (page 105) are great for mopping up the sauce.

HOW TO EAT WITH OTHER PEOPLE

These days when I organize a meal with a bunch of friends or my family, we have to consult everyone's dietary requirements before even thinking of what to eat, let alone where we're going to buy the produce.

In our age of individualism, there are so many different titles for what your food requirement could be, whether it's pescatarian, vegetarian, flexitarian, vegan, lacto-ovo, paleo, Atkins, fruitarian, I eat eggs but not duck eggs, I'll only touch it if it's all organically grown surrounded by nature and singing maidens, etc.

How can we even start to think about cooking something with pleasure if there's all these pressures and rules?

The thing is, I'm a culprit as well, given what I know about the industry. If I go to my parents' farm I'll be happy to eat roast pork every now and again (accompanied by mountains of veg) but if I go to a friend's house in London I'm definitely a veggie, as the meat they buy is probably not what I want to eat. I might go to a friend's house to eat their vegan meal which I am excited about until they whip out some soya-based plastic cheese, the sort that looks like it was from a school canteen in the 90s and is probably destroying rainforests in Bali to mass-produce soya. I was planning a once-a-year meal for a large gathering until I got the list that said I couldn't use eggs, dairy, gluten, meat, shellfish, chicken or sugar. It was definitely possible to cook something, in some ways a fantastic creative exercise, but how sustainable, seasonal and local it was, I have no idea.

The whole concept of dietary requirements came about because of allergies – because if a person ate a particular food they might be at risk of death. This is extremely unfortunate and I am sorry for those who have this – we have coeliacs come into the pub who have not eaten pizza for 10 years until we make one of ours. The joy and delight they express is rewarding for us both, but far more for them, I'm sure.

There are only two things that make good food – great produce and a happy cook. The cooks, chefs, friends who invite you round to dinner – whoever they are they should be made to feel excited about cooking for you. Yes, have an ethos, yes, have morals, or individual needs and desires but don't let them get in the way of a happy cook who is putting their love and energy into making something for you. Giving back the love to the cook will only inspire and promote more great cooking. If you need to give your requirement, give it in a way that is easy for them to understand... the simpler the title the better.

Likewise, choosing a restaurant when eating out is just as hard as we usually have no idea how honest the restaurant is, or where they get their produce from. There is a growing movement within the industry to make things more transparent so our customers know where all the ingredients are from. The Sustainable Restaurant Association is the leading organization in the UK trying to help restaurants to operate with more sustainability – they reward for many different areas including provenance, resources, staff, community, waste and local food. If you want a restaurant you can trust, then ask these guys. Look out for their logo. You, the customer, need to regain your trust in food establishments.

Above all, share your love for food and your knowledge of how to cook sustainably. Recipes are for sharing – that's why there are cookbooks! Share yours, share your local gems of produce and your favourite local restaurants.

Sweetcorn and Courgette Fritters with Salsa, Split Pea Hummus and Slaw

SERVES 4

FOR THE HUMMUS

250 G/9 OZ/1⅓ CUPS DRIED SPLIT PEAS

3-4 GARLIC CLOVES, CHOPPED

50 G/1¾ OZ/⅓ CUP ROASTED LINSEEDS

JUICE OF ½ LEMON

250 ML/8½ FL OZ/1 CUP COLD-PRESSED OIL

SALT

FOR THE SALSA

2 RED PEPPERS

1 RED ONION, THINLY SLICED

1 RED CHILLI, THINLY SLICED

HANDFUL OF PARSLEY, FINELY CHOPPED

DRIZZLE OF OIL, SQUEEZE OF LEMON JUICE AND PINCH OF SALT, TO SERVE

FOR THE FRITTERS

2 COURGETTES (ZUCCHINI)

2 SWEETCORN COBS

100 G/3½ OZ/¾ CUP BROAD BEAN (FAVA BEAN) FLOUR

HANDFUL OF FRESH PARSLEY, CHOPPED

1 EGG (OPTIONAL)

HIGH SMOKING POINT OIL, FOR FRYING

FOR THE SLAW

2 BEETROOTS

1 CARROT

HANDFUL OF FRESH CORIANDER (CILANTRO) STALKS AND LEAVES, FINELY CHOPPED

PINCH EACH OF ZA'ATAR AND GROUND CUMIN

DRIZZLE OF OIL, SQUEEZE OF LEMON JUICE AND SPICY SEEDS (PAGE 13), TO SERVE

Soak the split peas in plenty of cold water for at least 6 hours or overnight before using.

For the hummus, cook the split peas in a large saucepan of simmering water for 40–45 minutes until they are soft. Drain and transfer to a food processor. Add the garlic, roasted linseeds and lemon juice and blitz. Slowly pour in the oil with the food processor running until it's smooth in texture, then season with salt. Refrigerate until needed.

Preheat the oven to 180°C fan/200°C/400°F/gas mark 6.

For the salsa, roast the red peppers whole in the hot oven for about 30 minutes until they're caramelized and soft. Remove and immediately put in a separate bowl and cover with a plate. Leave for 20 minutes, then peel the skins off. Remove the seeds and stalks as well. Slice the roasted peppers and place in a serving bowl with the sliced red onions, chilli and chopped parsley. Mix together with oil, lemon juice and a little salt to make a salsa. Set aside.

For the fritters, grate the courgettes and then squeeze them in a colander to drain excess water. Place in a mixing bowl. Remove the sweetcorn kernels by running a knife down the sides of the cobs, then add these to the bowl along with the flour, a pinch of salt and the parsley. If you're not vegan, then add the egg to help the mixture bind. Mix together, adding a bit more water or flour until the mixture holds together nicely. Shape into fritters, about 5-cm/2-inches in diameter and leave on a board to one side.

For the slaw, grate the beetroot and peel and grate the carrot. Mix the chopped fresh coriander with the salt, za'atar and ground cumin. Drizzle with oil and lemon juice and mix. Top with some Spicy Seeds. Set aside.

When you're ready to serve, put a frying pan (skillet) on a low-medium heat with a good helping of oil. Place some fritters into the pan, being careful not to overcrowd it, and allow them to sizzle and cook for a 4–5 minutes. Once golden, turn over and continue to cook on the other side. When the fritters are dark golden all over, remove from the pan with a slotted spoon and drain excess oil. Repeat with any remaining fritters until they are all cooked.

Now serve your dishes down the middle of a table, ready for you and all your guests to build your own pyramids of flavour and texture. Natural yogurt would also be a great addition here.

25

THE BIGGEST ELEPHANT IN THE ROOM

Let's really talk about
the elephant in the room.
Overpopulation.

The Green Revolution

Population growth has steadily increased since the 1750s for a number of reasons, including the Industrial Revolution, better medical care, a decrease in child mortality, better hygiene and, more recently, the agricultural revolution known as The Green Revolution. The Green Revolution transformed food production, saving millions from famine and increasing profit and GDP per capita. It did this by developing seeds to make crops more resistant to diseases, instigating modern irrigation projects and making pesticides, herbicides and fertilizers widely available. It has saved billions of lives.

Side note: the name Green Revolution is nowadays slightly ironic given its widespread introduction of mass marketed pesticides and synthetic fertilizers, and new seed development which created monoculture farming.

Since the Green Revolution, it is estimated that the world population has grown by about 5 billion. To match this growth, our calorie production has increased but the quality and nutrition of those calories has decreased, resulting in what some could say was a far less efficient farming method. Today, malnutrition is one of the largest causes of death. Even in the UK where we have an abundance of food, obesity, diabetes and other food-related diseases are some of our most challenging problems. To what extent are the results of the Green Revolution now killing huge numbers of people? If the UK didn't have the NHS, how many lives would diabetes, obesity and other food-related problems have taken?

Norman Borlaug, who was dubbed 'the Father' of the Green Revolution should be given the right respect for what he did at the time – his new systems helped save people. But even he said 'The Green Revolution has won a temporary success in man's war against hunger and deprivation; it has given man a breathing space. But the frightening power of human reproduction must also be curbed; otherwise the success of the Green Revolution will be ephemeral only.'

He recognized that population growth had to stop.

An infinite system in a finite world

This is THE reason that the capitalist system we have now cannot work. How can you have an infinite system where there is no end to our species or capabilities, within a finite world of resources? English economist and demographer Thomas Malthus predicted that humankind would outgrow its available resources, because a finite amount of land would be incapable of supporting a population with a limitless potential for increase.

This all sounds very scary but it doesn't have to be the way. Remember Farmer Spud and Mr Crisp (page 20) – the end result didn't have to be wasted on excess gas and heat. They had the option to create a more efficient business that reinvested their waste into generating more calories or energy for humankind.

There is more than enough food in the world for humans to survive, we've just got caught up in an extremely inefficient system. We already grow enough food for 10 billion people but the world is malnourished, and the food we make is dispersed badly. So, the bigger questions at hand are: how can we use the land more efficiently and how can we create food more efficiently?

The efficiency of capitalism

Only 2% of the UK's labour force grows food. If the state crumbled and we were forced to feed ourselves, more people could do it. If we had to give up a few privileges to grow food ourselves to feed a nation, it could be done.

But do we want to give up these privileges? Ahh... that's a different question.

'Some polls from the UK found that 37 percent of all British workers think their job is completely useless.'
– Rutger Bregman, *Utopia for Realists*

Although this statement seems a bit harsh, we should question whether our current systems are conducive to producing human happiness. In the increasingly tough world where so many of us are living hand to mouth, just about surviving day to day, is it possible to change your ways to make a better world? It is very difficult to make these changes. And remember it's not all your fault we're in this situation.

Zero waste is one of the three key principles in this book, so maybe we should think about applying this ethos across all industries. Surely we don't want to be wasting our own energy on jobs that we perceive as useless – the calories we ingest shouldn't be wasted, but instead should be put to good use, whether it's growing food, making the community better, helping those in need or anything that helps the human race. Are we actually using our land as efficiently as possible? Could we be growing more in less land space, organically? Are there more constructive jobs that could be created that contribute towards the survival of humankind? Perhaps we need a community day each week when people have to add something to society?

Grass roots

So why is any of this related to the title: 50% of produce within 30 miles? Let's see if the trees can help us...

Trees are incredible organisms. I love them and I'm definitely not a tree-hugging hippy – nothing against them. We are completely dependent on trees' ability to turn carbon dioxide into oxygen for us to breathe. They're beautiful and magnificent and live for hundreds of years, providing shelter and food for lots of species. And what do they ask for? Not a lot... the sun, water and CO2. Without them life would be bleak.

Humans can sometimes have a visually singular perspective on nature; I mean this in the artistic sense. When we look at trees, we literally see just the trees. But if we examine closer, we would begin to see all the other tiny worlds going on – the mice that live in the roots, the mould growing on bark, the insects around the leaves. And underground, we would find earwigs and beetles, maybe truffles and rotting leaves, but most importantly mycelium. Mycelium is a collection of thin-thread organisms. I mentioned at the beginning of the book that the largest organism in the world was a mushroom... well, more specifically it's the mycelium. They're like the natural internet. A web of organisms where information and energy are transferred. What makes trees so strong is how effective their mycelium is at linking the roots of different species, sharing nutrients like nitrogen, helping to suck up water and sharing information to help immune systems.

Dr Suzanne Simard, who has given a TED speech on this subject, says, 'These plants aren't really individual in the sense that Darwin thought... in fact, they're interacting with each other, trying to help each other to survive.'

Look how wonderfully connected and social a tree is. This is what we all could be like if we grew our economies and societies like this. The more we buy local, the more social and globally connected we are as a species, then the stronger we will be going into the future.

Buying 50% of your produce from within 30 miles isn't a restaurant tagline, it's a future for our species. Be strong locally and connected globally.

How does this help population growth?

Good question... perhaps we're coming to the end of our population growth rate anyway? So why change?

I guess the question I'm posing is whether we are going to prove efficient enough as a species to ensure our own continuing survival? What are we evolving towards? How can we slow growth morally? Let's finish this chapter with the knowledge that local business can make us stronger and more connected. And that condoms are just as important as any of this.

'You know, when we first set up WWF, our objective was to save endangered species from extinction. But we have failed completely; we haven't managed to save a single one. If only we had put all that money into condoms, we might have done some good.'
— Sir Peter Scott, Founder of the World Wide Fund for Nature, *Cosmos* magazine, 2010

Mushrooms on Toast with Poached Eggs

As we've been talking about mycelium and mushrooms, it's only appropriate to have a recipe that celebrates them. The thing with mushrooms is that there's so much air in them, so they absorb whatever they've been cooked in. We're going to caramelize them down here so that they lose that spongy texture and gain wonderful flavour.

SERVES 2

3-4 TBSP VINEGAR OF YOUR CHOICE

COUPLE OF SLICES OF SPELT SEEDED BREAD (PAGE 102)

OLIVE OIL OR BUTTER, FOR FRYING

250 G/9 OZ MUSHROOMS, SLICED

2 EGGS

SALT

HANDFUL OF CHOPPED FRESH CHIVES AND CHIVE FLOWERS, TO SERVE

First, bring a saucepan of water to the boil and add the vinegar. (To achieve perfectly poached eggs, as long as your eggs are as fresh as can be you don't need to do anything other than just gently crack each egg in the vinegary water and leave for about 3 minutes.) We'll poach the eggs later, just get the boiling water ready now.

Place some glugs of oil or a good spoonful of butter in a frying pan (skillet) with the mushrooms. Turn the heat to medium and let the mushrooms start to caramelize for 5 minutes. If they are browning too quickly, then turn the heat down a little. Water is a great tool to allow them to cook for longer without burning, so once they have coloured to your liking, add 100 ml/3⅓ fl oz/⅓ cup of water and let reduce until there is no liquid left. Season with salt.

Meanwhile, toast the bread and butter it. Poach your eggs for 3 minutes and drain. Divide the fried mushrooms between the pieces of toast and nestle an egg on top of each. Scatter with chives and the beautiful purple chive flowers to finish.

26

LOCAL BUSINESS

Now we've decided to live like mycelium, strong locally and connected globally, we should explore our local area as much as possible. Imagine we're exploring the tree like on page 134, finding those truffles.

If we live within 30 miles, then we're going to want to make those 30 miles amazing! Have you ever heard of urban Honey? It is estimated that there are 5000 beehives in London alone, meaning that at the height of summer, honeybees outnumber humans in London by 30 to 1. London honey can be delicious – Greater London honey won first prize at the 2003 National Honey Show. I guess this is because of the variety of flowers and trees within an urban area as opposed to rural farms that grow single varieties of crops.

But now imagine how good it would be if we all cycled more and there was less pollution. Imagine how delicious honey could be if we spent more time looking after the communal flowers and planting a mixture of species. Imagine how beautiful our cities would look if we created a better space for our bees, so nature could flourish.

Eating locally means you are investing in the area you live in – it could attract better restaurants to open there, independent shops to really thrive and even ultimately increase house prices.

TWO BEAUTIFUL BRUSCHETTAS WITH HONEY

Peach, Blue Cheese, Honey, Walnuts

Peaches are to blue cheese what Bonnie is to Clyde. Strong and unique individually, but (drizzled with lashings of honey) together something even more powerful. This delicious combo will never get old.

SERVES 1

8 WALNUTS IN SHELLS, DESHELLED

2 SLICES OF SPELT SEEDED BREAD (PAGE 102)

100 G/3½ OZ LOCALLY PRODUCED BLUE CREAMY CHEESE

2 RIPER THAN RIPE PEACHES, SLICED

LOCAL HONEY, FOR DRIZZLING

Preheat the oven to 200°C fan/220°C/425°F/gas mark 7.

Spread the walnuts out on a baking sheet and roast them in the oven for 10 minutes. Remove from the oven (leaving the oven on) and cool slightly before roughly chopping.

Toast the bread. Place the toast on a baking sheet and cover with the blue cheese. Place in the oven for 5–10 minutes to melt the cheese. Remove the toast from the oven and transfer to a plate. Place the sliced peaches on top, drizzle with honey and scatter with the roasted walnuts to finish.

Smoked Trout, Honey, Truffle Oil and Crème Fraiche

I first tried this flavour combination in a small tapas bar in Barcelona. Its sweet, smoky, creamy, sharp, earthy, savouriness blew my mind. Truffled honey is a wonderful product if you can find some locally, but using sustainable honey mixed with truffle oil is just as good.

SERVES 1

2 SLICES OF SPELT SEEDED BREAD (PAGE 102)

2 LARGE TBSP CRÈME FRAICHE

150 G/5½ OZ SMOKED TROUT

LOCAL HONEY, FOR DRIZZLING

TRUFFLE OIL, FOR DRIZZLING

SMALL HANDFUL OF FRESH DILL OR CHIVES, FINELY CHOPPED

Toast the bread. Spoon crème fraiche over the toast, then layer the smoked trout on top. Drizzle with honey and truffle oil. Finish with some dill or chopped chives. Smoked salmon is great for this too... and even better if you live by the sea.

Rhubarb, Honey, Yogurt and Cobnut Crumble

On its own, rhubarb has a face-scrunchingly sharp taste that can be too much for even the bravest of taste buds. But with just the right amount of sugar to soften its twang, its delicate sharpness becomes its best feature. It is a very seasonal crop but beautifully versatile, and can accompany anything from savoury mackerel or cheese to sweet frangipane or panna cotta. Lightly poaching the rhubarb in sugar is wonderful for the fruit itself, but you can also reserve any leftover liquid for use in cordials and other desserts.

SERVES 2

75 G/2⅔ OZ/¼ CUP LOCAL HONEY

25 G/¾ OZ/2 TBSP GOLDEN CASTER (SUPERFINE) SUGAR

300 G/10½ OZ FRESH RHUBARB, CUT INTO BATONS

FOR THE CRUMBLE TOPPING

30 G/1 OZ COBNUTS (OR OTHER LOCALLY SOURCED NUTS), ROUGHLY CHOPPED

50 G/1¾ OZ/½ CUP ROLLED OATS

1¾ TBSP UNSALTED BUTTER

25 G/¾ OZ/2 TBSP GOLDEN CASTER (SUPERFINE) SUGAR

2 SLICES OF BRIOCHE

2 LARGE TBSP NATURAL YOGURT

In a saucepan add the honey, sugar and 50 ml/1⅔ fl oz/3½ tbsp of water (if second quantities) and bring to a simmer. Add the rhubarb and simmer for 5 minutes, then remove the pan from the heat and leave to cool.

Preheat the oven to 160°C fan/180°C/350°F/gas mark 4.

For the topping, add the chopped nuts to a large bowl with the oats, butter and sugar and mix together. Spread out over a baking sheet and bake for 15 minutes. Remove from the oven and leave to cool.

Toast the brioche slices, then cover with a good heap of yogurt. Spoon the stewed rhubarb over the yogurt with drizzles of juice. Scatter the crumble on top. You may have some rhubarb and crumble left over... these can be both be stored (the rhubarb in the fridge) and used for another occasion.

27

A LITTLE HELP FROM OUR FRIENDS

It's hard to find the support or information to help us become more sustainable, but luckily things are improving and there are some wonderful people who have done a lot of the hard work for you. If you have any problems or questions, these guys will be willing to help in any way.

Firstly, family, friends and neighbours

If you have an apple tree, then share your apples or barter them. Go blackberry picking together and share the winnings. Offer to use your neighbour's glut of tomatoes in exchange for some homemade tomato ketchup. As a community we can help each other to become sustainable.

30 Food 30food.co.uk

This website is a follow up to this book. Keep informed about how to join the Food Revolution and how to become a sustainable ambassador of the world.

The Sustainable Restaurant Association thesra.org

Their vision is to be the intersection of the food service industry and the sustainable food movement. They're just the right mixture of carrot (locally sourced of course) and stick (FSC certified). Cajoling us to do more and celebrating it when we do. Look for their logo in windows or use their website.

Slow Food slowfood.org.uk

Slow Food is a global grassroots movement with thousands of members around the world that links the pleasure of food with a commitment to community and the environment. Founded in 1989 in Italy, it celebrates beautiful food made by people who really care, no matter how long it takes.

Truth Love and Clean Cutlery truthloveandcleancutlery.com

A guide to the world's truly exemplary organic, sustainable and ethical restaurants. Both online and in book form, it's the guide we should all be following, especially with Giles Coren behind the steering wheel.

OLIO olioex.com

OLIO is a free app that connects users who have food they don't want or need with neighbours living nearby would like it. It can also be used to share non-food items such as toiletries, kitchen appliances, books, clothes and toys. Everything shared on OLIO is free, and over 1 million people have joined so far.

Farm Drop farmdrop.com

Farm Drop is an online food delivery company that distributes locally sourced foods from farmers and fishermen to consumers.

Karma karma.life

Karma's ultimate mission is to ensure that great food is never wasted. The app connects surplus food from restaurants, cafés and grocery stores to consumers for a lower price. As a result, users eat great food for less and businesses receive an additional revenue stream – all while reducing food waste.

Wonky Veg Boxes wonkyvegboxes.co.uk

Up to 40% of vegetables can go to waste because they don't look right. This fantastic group rescues this surplus, delivers it to your door and donates 10% of the produce to charities and food banks around Leicester.

There should be more businesses like this all over the world!

THE TIP OF THE ICEBERG

We are at the tip of the iceberg of this movement. I think we're about to enter a new era of civilization – The Moral Renaissance. A super-creative period of time when innovation will go hand in hand with strong morals and ethics to help humans survive. This renaissance is coming, not just in the food sector, but across all sectors where there is trouble and disparity. In fact, I believe we've already started. Humans have already innovated to create milk from plants – but we need to make sure that these milks are sustainable. So, if you have oats near you, then make oat milk. If almonds grow near you, then make almond milk and share it with your friends. Instead of automatically using the one ingredient listed in a recipe, ask yourself if it's local first – normally you can find something similar in your area just as good (see below simple substitutions). Before replacing any of the following ingredients, be sure to check how to cook with them properly first.

Wheat flour
Spelt flour
Potato flour
Tapioca flour
Millet flour
Broad (fava) bean flour
Rice flour
Pea flour
Quinoa flour
Maslin flour
Chickpea (gram) flour
Oat flour
Cornflour
Rice flour
Rye flour

Spelt
Rice
Barley
Pearl barley
Quinoa
Couscous
Freekeh
Bulgur wheat
Naked oats
Farro
Rye
Corn
Millet
Buckwheat

Chickpeas
Broad (fava) beans
Lentils
Split peas
Butterbeans
Cannellini beans
Borlotti beans
Marrowfat peas
Badger peas
Kidney beans
Flageolet beans
Pinto beans

Purple sprouting broccoli
Kale
Russian kale
Cavolo nero
Spring greens
Chard
Rainbow chard
Brussel sprouts
Spinach
Nettles
Leeks
Broccoli
Asparagus
Kohlrabi leaves
Watercress
Courgettes (zucchini)
Green beans
Dandelion greens
Cabbage
Bok choy/pak choi
Carrot tops
Beetroot leaves
Collards
Turnip greens

Almonds
Cobnuts
Hazelnuts
Walnuts
Cashews
Pecans
Brazils
Cedar/pine nuts
Peanuts

Sunflower seeds
Linseeds
Pumpkin seeds
Chia seeds
Hemp seeds
Sesame seeds
Acorn seeds
Apricot seeds
Squash seeds
Courgette (zucchini seeds)

Peaches
Plums
Damsons
Nectarines
Apricots
Greengages
Apples
Pears
Quince
Medlars
Figs
Grapes
Rhubarb

Strawberries
Raspberries
Blueberries
Goji berries
Cherries
Gooseberries
Elderberries
Mulberries
Blackberries
Redcurrants
Blackcurrants
Cranberries

Onions
Shallots
Leeks
Celery
Spring onions (scallions)
Fennel
Carrots
Celeriac
Peppers

Celeriac
Swede
Turnip
Jerusalem artichoke
Salsify
Parsnip
Kohlrabi
Squash

OUR RIGHT TO EAT GOOD FOOD

I truly believe that everyone on earth has the right to eat good food. We are an intelligent, passionate and caring species – we all deserve the basics. I'm demanding a change in our society that means everyone has access to proper, organic food that supports individual health. One of the main aims for capitalism should be to provide this and currently it is not doing so. Austerity is a real thing and people are left malnourished when their only financial option is to buy cheap, non-organic, highly processed, low-nutrient food.

Zero waste

The government should step in and remove single-use plastic – we are the consumers, not the villain. But together we can all create a movement for the right people to hear our voice. Plant your own salad, make your calories count and eat the whole produce, whether it's a carrot or a chicken. Be creative!

Organic

Nature did not make organic a class or financial issue, the supermarkets and governments did. Organic is normal fresh produce, and always has been. Let's flip the coin and see it the other way around: everything else should be clearly marked as 'non-organic' or 'pesticide sprayed'. Organic farming helps to promote from the roots up, which means everything at the bottom of the pyramid is strong, holding the whole ecosystem together. Bees, insects and pollinators are so important to our lives – let's celebrate them and look after them. Organic tastes so much better, and, by using techniques in this book, you can afford it by cooking sustainably.

30% from 50 miles

Live and breathe your local area – find the best suppliers, explore the best restaurants that care and eat the tastiest local produce. Remember the mycelium – live locally, connect globally. Let's enjoy being part of the bigger picture, by making the local areas as good as they can be.

Trust

The sustainable diet is the healthiest diet for you and your country. It will help lower the money spent on health care, allowing governments to spend more on things you really want and need rather than fixing problems that could have been avoided. Look at how hard we're all working – we put so much energy into every day, you would expect that our lives would be easy, healthy and bountiful. So, what's going wrong? We're investing our energy in the wrong direction – all we need to do is change the direction of the train tracks and suddenly we're on the journey to happiness and survival.

We are entering, if we're not already, into a society that has no trust in anything; not in politicians, not in the economy, not in banks and especially not in the food industry. We need a cultural and societal revolution to bring back our trust – an honest and fair vision for a better future that helps everyone. Bringing it back to food, the reason why recipes are such a good tool for a change in direction is because they allow you, the people, to take control of what you're eating again. You grow it, you cook it, you eat it.

Love the Revolution. Trust what we eat.

LOVE

Love food, and love eating.

It's not scary, it works most of the time, sometimes it doesn't. Growing your own is rewarding and far more delicious and fresher than supermarket produce. If you haven't already, eat the salad you started growing on page 12. Taste the organic first, then taste the non-organic – that is, if you want to eat it after you've sprayed it. You are what you're eating is eating – loving the planet means loving yourself, your family, friends and everyone around you.

We're not preachers, we're lovers!

Love the slightly hard cheese in the back of the fridge that makes an amazing pasta

Love your friends for trying something new

Love what you're eating is eating

Love being part of something massive

Love the fact that a vegetable one year could taste better the next year

Love the wild produce that you need to hunt for

Love the vegetable bodies, no matter what shape

Love the knobbly wobbly carrots (and their tops)

Love the food from abroad

Love the fish that you can't see

Love the asparagus that only comes once a year for that short season

Love the people who don't know how to cook sustainably yet

Love sharing a homemade pizza with friends

Love the produce around us and love the food from abroad

Love the spice that turns yet another cauliflower into a thing of beauty

Love the cook who makes your food

Love picking your own fruits on a hot summer's day.

Love turning your leftovers into an even better meal the next day

Love the people who make your food